Items should be returned on or before the last date shown
below. Items may be renewed by personal application,
writing, telephone or by accessing the online Catalogue
Service on Fingal Libraries' website. To renew give date
due, borrower ticket number and PIN number if using
online catalogue. Fines are charged on overdue items
and will include postage incurred in recovery. Damage to,
or loss of items will be charged to the borrower.

TACKLING DEPRESSION

A Practical Guide to Everyday Coping

Ian Birthistle

KITE BOOKS

Published by Kite Books, an imprint of
Blackhall Publishing
Lonsdale House
Avoca Avenue
Blackrock
Co. Dublin
Ireland

e-mail: info@blackhallpublishing.com
www.blackhallpublishing.com

© Ian Birthistle, 2010
ISBN: 978-1-84218-196-6

Printed in Ireland by Colour Books Ltd.

Acknowledgements

I want to express special thanks to all those who supported me in this endeavour but especially to Elaine, who supported me most, and who has to listen to me more than anyone else.

Contents

Contents

Introduction

Depression is a word that we all know, but only those of us who have experienced depression truly know what it means. Depression is not something that we can just snap out of, or that will disappear if we concentrate on all the positive things in our lives. However, it is something that can lift, light can shine through the dark clouds and, as impossible as it may seem to us, we can do things in our lives that will help us to feel better.

As a counselling psychologist I treat depression but I have also suffered from depression throughout my life. Therefore, the views expressed in this book are based on my work and my own personal experiences. I have included narrations of a person's experience of depression at different stages in the book, in which depression is described as 'the dark cloak' or as a 'darkness'. These are based somewhat on my own personal experiences but mostly on my experiences through my work. They are intended to give an insight into the mind of a depressive at all stages of depression and recovery. The reader may identify with the feelings expressed.

Tackling Depression focuses on how to identify and deal with depression so that we can have a more content existence. It is aimed at all those who suffer from depression, from those who have only just accepted their difficulties to those who have spent years trying to manage this affliction. The areas covered are the most pertinent for any individual with depression.

After looking at the process of identifying the symptoms of depression (Chapter 1), I then examine the causes of depression (Chapter 2). The numerous ways we can feed our dark moods through our own actions and inaction, what we tell ourselves and how we perceive the world in general are explored in Chapter 3. Discovering these thought processes are essential to any recovery, as our best efforts to manage our moods will be in vain if we continue to feed our depression. The focus then moves to tackling depression and the many ways in which an individual can address their issues (Chapters 4–6). For this, I provide a unique and simple slant on cognitive therapy, which is considered by many to be the most effective way of treating depression. I have put together my own treatment model, which I have found to be effective in assisting myself and others (see Chapter 4).

Chapter 7 is devoted to a discussion of suicide, including a look at the myths surrounding this desperate act and the particular difficulties of bereavement due to suicide.

While writing this book I encountered a number of clients at work whose depression was directly related to the recession in Ireland. Unemployment, debt and the loss of one's lifestyle are triggers for depression in individuals (Chapter 8), and they indicate how economic hardship can adversely affect any individual. Of course, these triggers can exist independently of an economic downturn and with the same deleterious effects.

The final chapter, 'Continued Recovery', is of paramount importance as managing depression is an ongoing effort, albeit a less arduous one than dealing with deep depression.

Tackling Depression is written in a clear and concise fashion. I avoid psychological jargon. My intention is to make this book as user-friendly as possible so that people can gather the pertinent information without having to wade through dense text.

The book is laid out so that you can read from start to finish, which will bring you from the stage of identifying depression, through to recovery and the everyday management of depression. However, it is also a reference book that the reader can dip in and out of, depending on their own circumstances.

The book should also be of assistance to those who are living with a depressed individual, and who are struggling to understand and find ways to help and care for the depressive and themselves. People with depression can have a tendency to isolate themselves, so this book could be used as a conversation starter by a concerned person, or as a means to better understand what a depressive is feeling. Parents could use it with a withdrawn teenager, or couples as a way to begin communicating and connecting again. This book will give people a language with which to discuss depression, especially with those who may seem irretrievably lost.

Attitudes to depression are gradually becoming more receptive. Depression used to be viewed with much stigma and disgrace and the individual carried a humiliation that only added to their burden. An increasing number of people openly talking about their difficulties – including a number of people in the public eye – has done much to dispel the misconceptions that depression is disreputable, shameful and something that should not be talked about. This undoubtedly gives many the courage to address their problems in the search for a better life.

Even though the attitude to depression has improved significantly, it is still an affliction that can go very much unnoticed. The withdrawn teenager, the isolated farmer, the woman who always paints on a smile – these could be the natural states of individuals with no tendencies to depression, or, equally, they could be indicative of or hide an underlying pain. When people conceal their depression it can be very easy to overlook what they are suffering, but we may also refuse to notice our own depression, attributing it to a physical illness or mental inadequacy. I hope that this book gives many the chance to identify depression in themselves and to learn to manage their lives more effectively.

1

Identification

I wake into the best part of the day: the blissful few moments before I remember that I have been terribly depressed. I begin to wonder what sort of day this will be. I shudder, and wonder if my black cloak is waiting above me, ready to envelop and cover every pore of my body. I am frightened. What sort of person will I be today?

Will I be catatonic and remain motionless in my bed, afraid to face the outside world and just pull the duvet over my head in a vain attempt to evade my emotions? Perhaps I will fool myself that I am not as bad as yesterday, only to make it as far as the television, and to remain there, motionless, staring through the moving images into an abyss of nothingness?

Will it be one of those days when I fear that everyone can see through my eyes and deep into my being? Why can't they mind their own business and leave me alone?

Maybe it'll be one of those days when few can truly see me. When I can conceal my identity with polite pretence and people interact with me as if I am normal.

> *When I stand outside of myself and observe myself, I wonder how I do it. How can I function when I feel so bad? It's amazing how all these people are so wrong in that they see me as a positive and content individual.*
>
> *Perhaps it will be one of the very rare days when these heavy chains are cut from my back, and the substantial weight of despair lifts to reveal an oasis of pleasantness and appreciation of all that surrounds me.*
>
> *But the dark cloak takes less than ten seconds to begin to cover me. How will it affect me today?*

Feeling Sad

At certain points in our lives, all of us know what it is like to feel depressed. We may feel 'a bit down,' 'a bit blue,' 'somewhat melancholy', we may 'not be firing on all cylinders', we may feel 'off-colour', or have just 'retreated inside ourselves' and be just 'a bit quiet'. We have many ways of describing feeling depressed, and what this seems to signify is the varying degrees and strengths of this emotion.

To feel sad at times in our lives is perfectly natural; perhaps it is also essential. Many philosophers believe that in order for us to feel happy and content, it is also necessary for us to feel sad and depressed, for, otherwise, how would we know the difference? Our childhood years are saturated with feelings of happiness and sadness. We might have felt sad when our soothers were taken away, sad when our mothers put us down, sad when our ice cream fell on the ground and sad when we couldn't have something that we wanted.

Our feeling happy and sad and everything in between continues throughout our adolescence and into and throughout our adult years. Sadness can come with relationship break-ups, not getting exams, losing a job, the death of a loved one or dissatisfaction with how our lives are going. Again, all of this is perfectly natural, but such feelings are essentially transitory and are constantly changing.

When we talk about depression, we talk about a persistent low mood, an enduring dark place, an unshakable heaviness, a constant dejection and an unrelenting despair. It continues for an extended period of time. It can appear and disappear for no reason; it can envelop us when everything is going well and disappear without a trace. We feel subject to its whimsical stealth-like manoeuvres. It can feel like a force outside of our control, which only gets worse when we try to control it.

Some of us are painfully aware of our depression, while others can be stoutly resistant to any acceptance of this form of weakness and vulnerability. Others can suffer for years without any real awareness of their state of being or why their moods and psychological patterns can inexplicably change for the worse.

I never knew what was happening. To be honest, I didn't notice anything for years. I was too busy enjoying myself. I reckon my moods were obscured by constant activity, frequent nights out, new friends, exciting prospects for fun and endless pleasurable distractions. It wasn't until life slowed down considerably that I finally couldn't avoid how I felt.

I was on a roller coaster in the dark, hitting highs and lows without any warning, and then a period of unsettling calm before the next bout of uncontrollable sadness. I couldn't sleep, possessed with disturbing negative thoughts. I'd lose my appetite and interest in all activities. I'd lose hope and any meaning that I had in life. It was very frustrating; I couldn't understand why my moods were shifting so significantly for no apparent reason at all. The more I looked at and tried to fix how I felt, the more irritated and angry I got.

Those who were closest to me bore the brunt of my venom. Anger covered all my hurt and sadness, and it was this emotion that was expressed to and suffered by my closest relatives. I had no comprehension of any other feelings except a relentless misery inside me. Even if I did, I had no skills to access them in a safe manner and express them appropriately without harm to myself or others.

When I look back, I can see that I suffered from depression throughout my teenage years, yet they seem to have been much shorter periods of gloom. Perhaps this is just retrospect or maybe the constant activity and distractions of those years helped.

I remember feelings of desperation, anxiety, hopelessness, extreme fatigue for ordinary activities, no interest in pastimes and puzzling tears over 'split milk'.

Back then depression was not a word that was spoken out loud; it was seldom, if ever, referred to, and there was an emphasis on keeping your problems to yourself and just getting on with things. I have no doubt that this prevailing attitude to depression contributed to my ignorance of it, but also to how inadequately I was coping with my misery.

Clinical Diagnosis

There are many different classifications of depressive disorders, with different specifiers such as early or late onsets, catatonic or melancholic features, or seasonal patterns. In terms of postnatal depression, postpartum onset, for instance, lasts significantly longer and is much more severe than a 'Baby Blues' depression. There can be single or recurrent episodes of all types of depression. It could be in partial or full remission, or classified as mild, moderate, chronic or severe, with or without psychotic features. Diagnosis can become complicated, but to keep it simple we can divide the mood disorders into the following three categories:

1. Depressive Disorders
2. Bipolar Disorders
3. Medical and Substance-Related Disorders

Major Depressive Disorder

This is a depressed mood for two weeks or more, with five or more of the following symptoms in the same two-week period:

- Feeling depressed for most of the day
- Loss of interest in most activities
- Loss of energy; fatigue
- Weight loss or weight gain due to poor appetite or overeating
- Sleeping more or sleeping less
- Feelings of restlessness or being inactive
- Loss of or increase in libido
- Poor concentration

- Indecisiveness
- Feelings of worthlessness or inappropriate guilt
- Recurrent thoughts of death, not necessarily suicidal

The symptoms cause significant distress and impairment in everyday functioning, and they are neither due to the taking of a substance (drugs or alcohol) nor to grief over the death of a loved one, nor are they better accounted for by a medical or emotional condition such as anxiety or worry.

Another classification of a major depression is dysthymia, which is characterised by a mildly depressed or irritable mood, often accompanied by other symptoms. This can last at least two years.

Bipolar Disorder

This is characterised by one or more major depressive episodes, accompanied by at least one or more manic episodes. A manic episode is an abnormal and persistent elevated or irritable mood lasting at least one week, with three or more of the following symptoms (or four if the mood is only irritable):

- Decreased need for sleep
- Excessively talkative or feeling of pressure to keep talking
- Distractibility
- Rapid and disorganised or incoherent flow of thoughts and speech (known as a 'flight of ideas')

- Inflated self-esteem or grandiosity
- Increase in goal-directed activity (socially, at work or sexually) or restlessness
- Increase in potentially detrimental pleasurable activities (excessive spending, foolish investments or sexual indiscretions)

These symptoms cause significant distress and impairment in everyday functioning, they may necessitate hospitalisation and they are not due to substance abuse or a medical condition.

The symptoms are classified as *hypomanic* if they last at least four days and are not severe enough to cause significant impairment in everyday functioning.

Medical and Substance-Related Disorders

This final category contains only two mood disorders. One of the disorders is a direct consequence of a physical illness or a *general medical condition*, while the other is a *substance-induced disorder* or the result of medication, or the abuse of prescribed or illegal drugs. The mood is characterised by a depressed and/or an elevated or irritable disposition. Both disorders require evidence from a physical examination or laboratory findings, and they cause significant distress and impairment in everyday functioning.

Other Signs

There are many varied indicators that a person may be experiencing depression. Other signs of depression reported by depressives are listed below, although it is important to remember that these symptoms may also be a result of some other emotional or physical upset:

- Little to no experience of pleasure
- A range of negative emotions from anxiety to anger to discouragement to hopelessness to shame, etc.
- Fear of dying, fear of losing control, fear of going mad
- Crying more than usual
- Loss of sense of humour
- Feeling like a failure
- Sudden mood swings
- Victim mentality
- Difficulties thinking and remembering; being easily distracted
- Being overly sensitive
- Substance use or abuse
- Getting preoccupied by things; indecisiveness
- Ambivalence, passivity and/or excessive concerns
- Irrational or extraordinary fears
- Compulsive worry or anxiety
- Self-blaming; abnormal thoughts
- Bad personal hygiene
- Slowness of speech
- Sad appearance
- Overtiredness
- Dependence and/or withdrawal

- Escapism; avoidance
- Panic attacks or phobias
- Inability to sit still or to concentrate
- Feelings of unreality
- Dizziness and faintness
- Migraines or headaches
- Nausea; constipation; diarrhoea
- Chest pain; pounding heart
- Sweating; trembling
- Impotence or excessive sexual behaviour
- Eczema; skin problems
- Alopecia (hair loss)

Identifying depression can be a difficult task, especially when many of us can be hugely resistant to accepting anything that may be wrong with us. It is important to realise that it is not something that is wrong and that it is not a weakness; it is something that every person will experience at some stage of their lives, but some of us just experience it more often than others.

By identifying and accepting our depression, only then can we begin on our paths to recovery and learn to manage our lives in a more effective manner. Life can get better for us, but identification and acceptance are the essential first steps.

It wasn't until I was in a steady relationship that I finally had to face and accept my depression. I had fought this realisation with stubbornness and nonchalance, refusing to accept that I had this label which to me only signified a form of weakness.

A stereotype of men is that we are only allowed to feel happy or angry, while women are allowed all emotions except for anger. Although I knew that I had felt sad and hurt in the past, I had never spoken about any vulnerable emotion, or even accepted any to myself. I was taught that big boys don't cry and that men do not share or express feelings.

I had a huge conflict within myself. I was desperately sad, but in order to survive as a man I wasn't allowed to feel the way I did. Fighting my depression only made it worse as I became more distant and angry. I would isolate myself and avoid human contact for days, or I would pick fights; I was in turmoil, and I was creating havoc all around me.

I had no idea of how to deal with an emotional problem. There was no obvious reason for how I was feeling, so I couldn't change anything. But trying to just get on with things was just not working anymore.

It seems to be the case for many of us that relationships can bring up a lot of our issues, and this was certainly the case for me. My depression had become unbearable for my partner: my sadness, my isolation and my anger had all reached a crescendo and something had to give.

I remember arguing and trying to blame everything and everyone else. I was furious but I had no reason to be. I couldn't understand this, but I felt like I was holding on to my fury for dear life. I was afraid that if I let go of this anger I would collapse into pieces. Everything beyond my frustration was unknown to me; it was all that I knew.

I had run out of ideas and all that was left was to trust the notion that to accept and explore this concept of depression was the only thing that could help.

I could never have imagined how it felt to accept my problem and to make an appointment to see a professional. My rage dissipated immediately and a huge sense of relief and peace overcame me. The darkness left me, and for the first time in years I felt content and at ease with myself.

Although my journey was only beginning, this was a glimpse of how I was to feel as I went through therapy and I finally began to deal with my depression.

Summary

- Feeling sad is natural, but depression can seem unshake-able and persists over an extended period of time

- There are many differing diagnoses and classifications of depression

- Signs of depression are numerous and varied, and may also be a result of some other emotional or physical upset

2

Causes

Understanding Depression – A Historical View

Depression is not a modern day concept; it has always existed. Philosophers such as Hippocrates (460–377 BC) believed that melancholia was caused by an excess of black bile. Plato (427–347 BC) held that this sadness could be divinely inspired, or could result when the irrational soul severed its connection with the rational. However, Plato's pupil Aristotle (384–322 BC) believed that all physical and mental illness was rooted in man's physical structure. Cicero (106–43 BC) postulated that emotional factors could cause physical illness, while Aretaeus (circa AD 30–90) was the first to propose that emotional disorders were an extension or exaggeration of existing character traits.

With the growth of Christianity around the fourth century, many historians believe that people were again more willing to believe in superstition and supernatural explanations. Much of the earlier advancements in scientific learning stopped, with communication with the devil becoming the culprit for perceived madness.

From around the thirteenth to the sixteenth century, which includes the period of the Renaissance, the Church was under attack from changes in society and culture, and also from within, due to questioning of the vows of celibacy. The status quo was changing. However, this was also a time when mental disorders were equated with sin, and so psychological disorders became entwined with legal and religious issues. Where no cause for a disease could be found, it was assumed to be caused by the devil. In a climate in which hundreds of thousands of women and children were burned at the stake for witchcraft, almost all logical thinking about mental illness was swept away.

From around the beginning of the sixteenth century, questioning of the established order did re-emerge, perhaps due to an increase in trading among Mediterranean countries or the re-introduction of the more compassionate Hellenic learning by the Arabs. Hospitals were established for the treatment of the mentally ill, focus expanded into thinking about the unconscious and subtle processes. Astrology and palm reading were explored, and reports from newly discovered lands challenged many attitudes to life.

Robert Burton's *Anatomy of Melancholy*, which appeared for the first time in 1621, looked at the psychological and social causes that were associated with and seemed to cause melancholia, while Spinoza (1632–1677) focused on the inseparability of the mind and body, rejecting the idea that man possessed absolute free will.

Franz Joseph Gall (1758–1828) believed that character traits were related to the structure of certain localised areas within the brain. He also looked at the force of emotional and moral factors and the roles of social upheaval and isolation in mental illness.

Conflict with one's consciousness, dreams, an excessive preoccupation with the internal world and organic causes of depression were all explored until Sigmund Freud's (1856–1939) psychodynamic theory arrived during the 1890s and was viewed as completely novel.

Theories

There are many different theories as to what causes depression, but no definitive one. Varying combinations of relevant theories may help to explain one person's depression but not the next person's. As yet, they all remain as theories.

Biological and Physiological

Much of the genetic evidence of what causes depression comes from the study of identical and non-identical twins, but it is compounded by the many other physical, social and emotional factors that can influence depression. Because of this, researchers believe that a person's genes may guide the way they regulate emotions and respond to life issues, thereby facilitating depression to occur when other conditions are present.

Research has shown bipolar disorder to be highly heritable, but major depression to be only modestly so. Attention has focused on a dominant gene, chromosome 11 (Egeland et al., 1987), and more recently on chromosomes 13 and 22 (Badner and Gershon, 2002).

The following are some examples of biological and physiological theories of depression:

- *The Neurotransmitter Theory*: A *neurotransmitter* is a chemical substance that is important in transferring a nerve impulse from one single nerve cell (neuron) to another. This model initially focused on the levels of neurotransmitters in the body such as serotonin, dopamine and norepinephrine, but it has more recently begun to focus on receptor sensitivity to these neurotransmitters, where there is evidence of poor serotonin sensitivity in depression (Moore et al., 2000). Other research focuses on second messengers, which modulate a cell's sensitivity to neurotransmitters, and also on G-proteins, which help modulate activity in the postsynaptic cell (receptor cell).

- *Brain Imaging Studies* suggest that episodes of depression are associated with changes in many of the brain systems, like the reward system, which is associated with the increase or decrease in a person's motivation to pursue rewards. Other research has also shown elevated responsiveness and diminished activity in various parts of the brain, but because these systems are so complex it is still unclear how depression relates to brain activity.

- *The Neuroendocrine System* is the biological system that manages reactivity to stress, and it can be overly active when people are depressed. It triggers the release of cortisol, the main stress hormone that initiates changes that help prepare the body for threats. High levels of cortisol are seen in many different psychiatric disorders, maybe as a reaction to the stress of these conditions.

Social Factors

That stressful life events trigger episodes of depression is a well-established fact, although debate does continue on whether the life events cause the depression or whether the depression was there already. Events such as the end of a romantic relationship or a key friendship, losing a job or a humiliation of some sort have been reported by many people as occurring in the year preceding the arrival of their depression. However, why is it that some people become depressed as a result of these experiences while others do not?

The theory is that there are pre-existing vulnerabilities (diatheses) that interact with certain stressors. Interpersonal research (research focused on people's interactions with and reactions to other people) highlights diatheses such as low social support, critical or hostile comments or emotional over-involvement by a family member with the depressed person, a great need for reassurance and poor social skills as representing the potential for depression in individuals.

Examples of the above have been found in many different studies. One analysis found that women experiencing a severely stressful life event without close support had a 40 per cent risk of developing depression, while those who had the support of a close confidant had only a 4 per cent risk (Brown and Andrews, 1986). This highlights the vital process of opening up and the essential role of social support in remaining emotionally and mentally well.

Research has shown married women as suffering more from depression than unmarried women or widows, with the reverse being true for men. For married women, depression may result from marital disharmony, while for unmarried men the reasons many relate to the difficulty of isolation or regret at not having a close bond with another.

Studies have found that the likelihood of becoming depressed increases if you are in a difficult social situation, such as if you lose your job. Using unemployment as an example, other variables such as your self-esteem, or whether, for instance, as a male you pride yourself on being the breadwinner, can further increase your chances of becoming depressed.

Other social factors such as isolation, homelessness, insufficient funds to support your family, bullying or discrimination can also increase the likelihood of you becoming depressed.

Why me? What did I do to deserve this? Other people seem to be able to manage the same difficulties but I'm falling apart. I wonder if I could find the cause then maybe I could change how I feel. I suppose it's obvious that if I find work and I'm in a good relationship then I will feel better, but will that be enough?

I was depressed before when I had a steady job and my mood didn't permanently lift even though my last relationship was very positive. It's more complicated than that. I wish there was some obvious cause for my depression that I could focus on so I could make myself feel better, but it's such a mystery.

Maybe it's in my genes or it's my unique psychological makeup.

Is it a hormonal imbalance? Is there something wrong in my brain? Is it my life's circumstances? Has it got to do with my childhood, my difficult upbringing and my dysfunctional family? Is it the way I think and how I perceive the world in general? Is it that I have little faith and no hope of things getting better? Have I sinned in a past life and now I have to pay for it? Is it some burden that I have to carry, like a test that I have to pass in order to experience the bliss of contentment?

The frustration of not knowing has me thinking of the most obscure possibilities. I am so confused! I wish I could fix this. I wish I could figure this out. I want to feel better.

Psychological Theories

There are many psychological approaches to depression; the biological approach has been discussed previously in this chapter and what follows are the most influential psychological theories on depression.

- *Psychodynamic Theory* suggests that people with especially strong dependency needs are most likely to develop depression. Sigmund Freud theorised that if a child's needs were insufficiently or overly gratified during a stage of childhood development that he called the oral period then the potential for depression was created. The child, when they grew up, would become fixated on this stage of life, causing them to become excessively dependent on other people to maintain their self-esteem. If the person was then to experience the death of a loved one or abandonment, Freud asserted that he or she would unconsciously resent being deserted and subsequently feel anger, which in turn would be directed inwards and develop into ongoing self-blame and depression.

- *Behavioural Theory* recognises that people become depressed due to social factors that lead to the loss of important rewards and reinforcements, such as becoming unemployed and losing your wage and position in life.

Cognitive Theories

Cognitive theories focus directly on the mental processes of how the brain takes in information and generates patterns of behaviour based on memory, judgement, decision making and similar functions. Cognitive theories are the most common focus of research on depression since negative thoughts and beliefs are seen as being major causes of depression. In the treatment of depression and anxiety, cognitive therapies are now seen as being at least as effective as anti-depressants; this is now well established and no longer subject to major debate. Cognitive therapy will be dealt with in more detail in Chapters 3 and 5; what follows are some of the best examples of cognitive theories.

Beck's cognitive behavioural theory (Beck, 1967) focuses on the impact of negative thinking (see Chapter 5 of this book). Through stressful childhood events such as rejection by peers, loss of a parent or the depressive attitude of a parent, depressed people acquire negative schemata. Not only is this a tendency to see the world negatively, but is also an unconscious set of beliefs, activated whenever the person encounters particular situations or negative events. Once activated, these schemata cause cognitive biases, which are tendencies to be overly attentive to negative feedback and information, and this in turn causes depression. According to Beck, a depressed person's schemata are maintained by the following three cognitive biases:

- *Arbitrary inference*: drawing negative conclusions in the absence of sufficient evidence
- *Selective abstraction*: drawing negative conclusions by focusing on one element while ignoring many other elements
- *Overgeneralisation*: drawing negative sweeping conclusions on the basis of a single and perhaps trivial event

The question does remain whether certain cognitive styles cause depression, or whether depressive symptoms cause those cognitive styles.

Helplessness Theory

This theory is based on Martin Seligman's (1974) learned idea of helplessness, which shows that animals acquire a sense of helplessness when confronted with uncontrollable aversive situations. When this was applied to humans, it was found that aversive experiences triggered helplessness in some people but not in others. Weiner et al. (1971) identified three key dimensions of how people understand the causes of stressors in their lives:

- Internal (personal) versus external (environmental) causes
- Stable (permanent) versus unstable (temporary) causes
- Global (relevant to many life domains) versus specific (limited to one area) causes

This addition to helplessness theory suggests that depression develops in people who believe that negative life events are due to internal, stable and global causes.

Albert Ellis's Rational Emotive Behaviour Therapy (REBT)

REBT proposes that we mainly feel the way we think. Ellis asserts that all psychological upset is based on a set of irrational beliefs, which when combined with a particular event would lead us to feel ill at ease. Our irrational beliefs would need to be identified and then challenged to form more rational beliefs, and subsequently we would feel better.

Ellis purports that we do not become depressed by certain events, but we become depressed by how we view these events. This is linked to other theories that anxiety and depression are caused when a person's core beliefs about the world are undermined. This can leave a person shattered and feeling that existence is devoid of meaning.

Attachment and Childhood Experiences

Early childhood experiences can leave a mark on a person's life, which can create a vulnerability to depression in adult life. Many theorists accept that faulty parent–child relationships lay the foundations for depression in later life. Studies have shown that the death of a parent, severe illness, an abusive upbringing, or abandonment and rejection by a parent can be influential in an individual becoming depressed in later life.

Many of these issues can cause a person to be stuck in the past. This can result in undeveloped and *inadequate coping mechanisms* that may have worked as a child but in adulthood are ineffective in dealing with depression, and may sometimes even exacerbate the problem.

For example, ignoring and suppressing emotions as a child in an abusive situation may be necessary for survival. However, in adult life, the attempts to disengage from various emotions may require behaviour such as addiction, which in turn would lead to depression. In essence, the attempts to suppress certain emotions may only lead to depression. Expression of our emotions is often the release that is needed to free us from the restrictiveness of our depression.

These early experiences can also leave us with a strong feeling of inadequacy. This feeling of being 'not good enough' can create depression in itself, but it may also encourage other depression-developing behaviours in our attempts to feel better.

For example, in order to feel good about ourselves, we may believe that we must perform well at a given task or that we must be liked by other people. We may come to value ourselves for how we compare to others in the performance of a particular job, or for how we believe we are perceived by others. This, however, is a recipe for disaster:

- To rate ourselves entirely on a particular task is not only incomplete, but we also give ourselves no allowance for an off-day. Therefore, this attempt to feel worth exclusively in terms of ability and achievement will not work, and is sure to result in us feeling depressed

- To rate ourselves entirely on how well liked we are by others, we must therefore become adept at pleasing people. We will lose our individuality by trying to become what we think people want us to be, and will therefore sabotage our relationships by losing the appeal of our individuality. We take no account of people who don't show approval, or who are having a bad day. We devote a lot of energy to living other people's lives while neglecting our own needs and desires. Some people are bound to disapprove of us, so this excessive need for approval will lead us to depression unless we accept how things really are

The lack of a strong bond between child and parent can increase a propensity for depression in the child in later life, with dysfunctional early childhood experiences possibly affecting relationships in adulthood. Through learned feelings of mistrust, fear of intimacy, fear of being hurt or perceived inadequacy, an individual may unconsciously form similar dysfunctional relationships in a vain attempt to mend childhood relationships. In addition to this, they may also struggle to form rewarding healthy relationships in which they can grow, and have difficulty learning to resolve situations that can lead to depression.

I have spent so much time looking for the cause of my depression. This frustrated me so much that it did contribute to my overall misery. For me, there was no one cause and my futile attempts to pinpoint one fixable source only left me exhausted, angry and depressed.

However, all was not in vain. During counselling, the excursions into my psyche highlighted relevant areas that helped me to feel much lighter and less depressed. I have learned that depression is to be managed and not fixed; trying to eradicate the emotion is impossible and I know that trying to do this in the past only set me up to be disappointed. It is possible not to plummet into as much darkness as I used to live in, but sadness is an emotion that all of us experience at different times and this just has to be accepted. It's strange, but this acceptance seemed to ease my uncomfortable emotions. It's like I gave myself permission to feel and that gave me the relief I was looking for.

I searched for a cause of my depression so that I could fix it. This did highlight some important and relevant issues that, when dealt with through therapy, did lighten my mood. But the answer that I was looking for was sitting under my nose. I believed that finding a cause would give me the tools to fix things, but I now realise that acceptance of how I felt was what I really needed. The answer is not always to fix and change. Sometimes two plus two doesn't always equal four; sometimes the answer is that 'I feel sad' and that is all that I need to understand.

Other Causes

There are many theories on the causes of depression, ranging from chemical imbalances in the body, to negative thought patterns and feelings, to the emotional turmoil that we can suffer as a result of other people's behaviour. Numerous combinations of certain theories can be relevant for any individual at any given time.

For example, some theorists believe that neuroticism, a personality trait that involves the tendency to react to events with greater than average distress and worry, predicts the onset of depression. A very self-critical individual runs a high risk of becoming depressed, as does a person with high dependency needs.

Depression can be a factor for people suffering from a diagnosed or undiagnosed mental illness. People with various forms of addictions can report their behaviour as an attempt to self-medicate for the effects of depression, but many also report depression as a result of their addictions.

Depression is a natural reaction to the death of someone close. However, with some people it can persist into becoming a major clinical depression. The end of a relationship can also trigger depressive tendencies that can develop into an enduring darkness, depending on how intimate the relationship was and how long it lasted.

People suffering from a form of abuse, whether in the past or present, often report an ongoing depression from present circumstances, or from triggers that elicit memories and feelings from the past. Difficult family issues are also seen by therapists as core issues related to a client's depression.

The prevalence of depression in society far outweighs any other psychological disorder, so perhaps this is a symptom of the capitalistic lifestyle that so many of us are immersed in. Some believe that depression is a search for answers, or perhaps even a manifestation of the dissatisfaction that many of us experience in life. People can struggle for meaning in life and this can lead to an existential quandary or spiritual crisis. People might feel let down by previously accepted religions, and can realise that they have little belief in what they have formerly held to be true. This fear of the unknown and the search for an understanding of life can be fraught with fear and subsequently develop into a lasting depression.

We can spend much time searching for our own depressive triggers in a vain attempt to address the cause and fix the depression. Most of us, if not all of us, experience this as a futile endeavour that only triggers an increasing frustration, which makes us feel even more hopeless in our depression.

Depression is different for all of us. It does not have an identifiable cause that can be fixed and mended. It is about our actions, our inactions, our reactions, our values, our beliefs, our thinking, our feelings; it is about our past, our present and our perceived future.

As will be seen in the coming chapters, there are certain things that we can do in order to greatly reduce our feelings of depression. These can vary from opening up and discussing significant issues from our past, to changing our way of thinking and our view of the world at large. What needs to be done will vary for each individual, but before we can make any of these changes we must first know ourselves better, and identify what our issues are and how we are feeding our negative emotions.

Summary

- There are many different theories on the causes of depression, but no definitive one

- Biological, physiological and psychological causes, as well as social factors and childhood experiences, can all have an influence on a developing depression

- Certain theories like cognitive and behavioural theories, and attachment and childhood experiences, may be more influential than others. However, a unique combination of theories usually helps to explain any given person's depression

3

Feeding Depression

Actions and Consequences

If I don't go to work, if I study for an exam, if I drink too much, if I try to change the unchangeable, if I exercise regularly, if I ignore my partner – each of these behaviours has either negative or positive consequences and by choosing the behaviour I therefore also choose to live with the consequences.

If I maintain an unhealthy relationship where I am excluded and snubbed, then I will probably become upset. So, in essence, I then choose to sadden and distress myself. If I insult a violent man then he'll probably beat me up. Again, I might as well just ask him to beat me up.

When I leave my house and I go left, there is a whole set of different consequences compared to if I go right. Life is made up of thousands of choices every day, and with every one of these choices comes a set of consequences. The trick is to become aware of the possible consequences before making our choices.

Our moods can be hugely affected by the choices that we make in life. We can delude ourselves into thinking that we are making an easy choice, or that the path of least resistance is the better road to travel. However, the consequences of these choices need to be examined because it's these consequences that affect our moods and create our own personal atmosphere in which we must live. In a nutshell – we choose how we feel by what we do.

This is paramount in understanding depression, because we can feed our depression and make it worse by what we do, or by what we don't do. The influence and effects of this will be different for each individual, and it can change over time for us all, so we need to be consistently aware of the consequences of our actions and our inactions. By becoming more responsible for our actions we can have an influence on the consequences, and this will affect our lives.

It is true that no one really understands how a depression is created. As noted in Chapter 2, there are many theories as to what causes depression and these can vary and differ significantly between individuals. What we do know is that we can make our depression worse or better by what we do or don't do in life, and also by how we think about life and ourselves in general.

Inactivity

We can often feel sorry for ourselves in our depression, and where, on the one hand, this is perfectly natural and understandable, we must also be careful that it doesn't take over and render us immobile. If we allow this self-pity to exist for too long, it can take us over like fast-growing ivy and choke us into static dejection.

Our depression constantly tells us exactly what to do and how to think in order for its misery to flourish. Inactivity feeds our depression, and this needs to be continuously challenged, as it is only through various forms of activity that we can eventually put ourselves on our paths to freedom.

We can fool ourselves into believing that when we feel the energy then we will make the effort to help our depression. But the problem is that, in order to feel the energy, we must first make the effort. Making the effort is probably the only thing that can defeat our depression.

I know what I need to do but yet I don't do it. I can struggle into work, but I fear the weekends. With no distraction from myself, my dark cloak begins to tighten around me. I feel panic and fear at what is ahead of me. Bank holiday weekends are worse, with more time to do nothing.

The conflict between what I want and what I need is perplexing. Stay in bed, don't go out, avoid all contact with people – my depression tells me that this will help, but I know that it is lying to me. I avoid this realisation, as to make any effort seems to require a phenomenal exertion worthy only of the great Hercules himself.

I want to feel the desire first, but here I am stuck in the depression conundrum. If I had the energy then I would make the effort, but what I can't deal with is that I must first make the effort in order to eventually feel the energy. Ah, fuck this.

My depression attacks this truth on all levels. My bones feel weary, depleted of any strength. I am subject to the laws of gravity that leave me lying on my bed. To speak requires an even greater strength – this power eludes me. I don't even have the energy to open my mouth. My thinking does have energy but it's purely negative, stuck like a broken record on one question: 'What's the point?'

Negative Actions

As mentioned above, what we do and don't do can have a huge effect on our depression. The consequences of our behaviour can very often lead to depression, or, on the contrary, our behaviour may also lead to an improvement in how we are feeling.

By paying attention to the emotional consequences of our actions, we can quickly become aware of what works and what doesn't work in helping us to feel more content. When the emotional consequence is more subtle, awareness can be gained by comparing and contrasting our moods that result from the same, similar and opposite behaviours.

If asked, most of us are able to name a number of activities that feed our depression. However, we can be quite resistant to bringing these behaviours out into the open. We may irrationally believe that these behaviours are of benefit to us in some way, or we may be very reluctant to let go of a behaviour that has become so familiar and subsequently so comforting.

There can be a payoff in depression in that some of us may actually enjoy being depressed, or it may be such a familiar way of being that any form of change is just too frightening. The drama of feeling low and the attractiveness of feeling sorry for yourself can become alluring and we can become immensely fearful of change. By naming depression-feeding behaviours, we identify not only ways of changing but also areas where effort needs to be directed.

By naming these behaviours, we decide not to hide behind what we could claim to be the powerlessness of our condition, and perhaps we take a step closer to deciding to change. Perhaps we are resistant to making the decision to change; be it out of fear of change or, perhaps, fear that our futile attempts will only make us more depressed.

Below is a list of behaviours and processes that depressives report can feed their darkness and make them feel worse:

- Going to bed late
- Getting out of bed late and missing the day
- Absence of sunlight
- Inactivity (physical and mental)
- Preoccupation with self
- Missing work
- Eating unhealthy food
- Indecision
- Watching too much television
- Isolation
- Avoidance, withdrawal and escapism
- Excessive alcohol
- Excessive drug use (illegal and prescription)

I lie in bed motionless. I wonder how I will feel today. I know that the longer I lie here, the more likely it is that my black cloak will wrap itself around me and I will find it harder to shake it off than if I get up now and do something. Ah, but I feel so tired and weary. I was up late watching **Star Trek** *repeats, and I've only had five hours* *sleep. The house is cold and the bed is warm. I'll have a quick snooze. I'll feel better then ....*

Oh no! It's two o'clock. I have three missed calls on my phone and one message from the lads looking for me to go to a match with them. Shit! I would really have liked that, but it's too late.

I get up. The house is a mess but I couldn't be bothered cleaning up or even cleaning myself. I know that I would feel better in a clean environment and clean skin, but I persuade myself that it's more important that I get some daylight as it will be dark in two hours' time, and then the day will be gone.

I dress in the same clothes as yesterday. I'm oblivious to the smell. I stand outside with my coffee and breakfast doughnut. I am rapidly going downhill. I am preoccupied with how bad I am beginning to feel, and it's becoming unbearable. I know what will help: going to the gym, doing some gardening, eating healthily, fixing the kitchen presses, reading, writing in my journal, visiting my family ....

I ignore my good advice on how to rescue the day. It's like I want it to fail as then I have a great excuse to engage in my favourite activity of doing nothing. I feel so bad now that it's only the beer that can ease my pain, but why am I drinking this stuff when I won't be able to drive any-where and I know that it's a depressant?

I turn on the television and settle into my favourite seat. It's Saturday so it's okay to watch a match on TV. I wonder how bad I will have to feel before I make the effort to change. How long will I continue like this?

Negative Thinking

As discussed in Chapter 2 under the heading 'Cognitive Theories', negative thoughts and beliefs are seen by many as the major causes of depression. This works on the premise that the more we tell ourselves something, the more likely we are to believe it. Subsequently, we will experience the feelings associated with a negative event, even though it hasn't happened yet. If I imagine something horrible happening in the present or future, I will begin to experience the emotions associated with that event as if it is happening or has already happened. For example:

- Imagining the death of someone you love will depress you very quickly
- Imagining your lover with another person will make you anxious and depressed
- Imagining a life of constant rejection and loneliness can leave you feeling utterly depressed and hopeless

When we look at this process objectively we can wonder why anyone would want to imagine such horrible occurrences, but the fact is that a lot of us do. We can be very unaware of our thinking, realising only that we feel depressed, but not that we have just fed that emotion with our negative thinking.

Cognitive Distortions

If we pay attention to our perceptions, our thoughts, our judgements, our assumptions and our self-talk, we may begin to notice a negative pattern or theme. Theorists refer to these negative thoughts as cognitive distortions – ways in which we negatively manipulate the facts and reality of what we experience in life. The consequence of this behaviour is to feel anxious and depressed, and is a very significant factor in how a lot of us feed our depression. Below is a list of such distortions:

- *Absolutist thinking*: this is sometimes referred to as black-and-white thinking, and it involves looking at the world in all-or-nothing terms and using ultimatum words in our thinking. For example, using absolute words such as 'always' or 'never', 'everyone' or 'no one', or 'everything' or 'nothing' can leave us feeling quite hopeless and depressed. The situation is probably less clear-cut than that and using more honest and rational terms, such as 'sometimes', 'some people' or 'some things', will result in us feeling less despairing

- *Selective abstraction*: this entails picking out a negative event and dwelling on it exclusively so that our view of reality becomes distorted and out of context. For instance, we can irrationally believe that there are only negative ways in which to view people and the world at large, or we can focus exclusively on everything that has gone wrong, ignoring positive aspects or things that we may have enjoyed

- *Emotional reasoning*: this is an assumption that our negative emotions reflect reality and that if we feel it, it must be true. For example, if I feel upset when my friend shouts at me, I may assume that he doesn't like me when it's just that he's worked up about something else. Or, again through my distress, I may assume that someone is annoyed with me if they don't say hello when I greet them, when the truth may be that they were so preoccupied that they didn't see me

- *Should statements*: the word 'should' is overused by us when we are mostly expressing a preference. When we direct a 'should' statement towards others, we are expressing anger or a judgement of them, but when used in our self-talk it is in the context of expecting ourselves to be perfect. Therefore, we feel disappointed, scolded and inferior. 'Shoulds', 'musts' and 'oughts' need to be changed to 'I would like' or 'I would have liked to'. The consequence of this is to feel motivated by these statements to ourselves rather than criticised and blamed

- *Overgeneralisation* (labelling and mislabelling): we can see a single negative event as something bigger than it actually is. For example, we can condemn ourselves as a person on the basis of a single event, or predict future disaster from a small mistake. Instead of rationally dealing with the negative event or mistake, we can attach a negative label to ourselves or others which is grossly exaggerated, and this emotionally loaded label results in us feeling depressed

- *Magnification or minimisation*: we may depress ourselves by overestimating the chances of disaster, exaggerating the negative consequences or importance of any particular event or reducing the positive until it has little effect. For instance, we can believe something small to have catastrophic consequences, while all the time concentrating so much on the negative that we minimise any of the positive

- *Disqualifying the positive*: the positive is discarded by paying attention only to the negative part of events; we can concentrate on our weaknesses while totally forgetting our strengths. By focusing on everything that has

41

gone wrong and forgetting or discounting things that we enjoyed or achieved, we come to believe that everything is negative and this can lead us to feel utterly hopeless

- *Personalisation*: like with emotional reasoning, we can believe that events or situations are directed at us personally, or we can see ourselves as the cause of a negative event when in reality it has little or nothing to do with us. For example, we may feel that a friend's mood is directed at us personally when it is merely an expression of something completely unrelated. Or we could blame ourselves for our depression when, in reality, it is not our fault

- *Arbitrary inference*: this is the result of basing what we think on poor evidence, confusing a thought with a fact and jumping to negative conclusions. We make negative life interpretations based on circumstantial information that would not be accepted as correct by other people. For instance, we can believe that people are thinking negatively about us, or that things will turn out badly, based on predictions and speculations that we believe are already well-established facts

Variations on cognitive distortions:

- *Brooding about the past*: the past may sometimes need to be looked at in order to let go of difficult issues, but dwelling on negative aspects of our past is a guaranteed way to depression

- *Asking questions that have no answers*: 'Why is life so unfair?' 'Why aren't things different?' 'Why does this always happen to me?' If they can't be turned into answerable questions, then it is best to let them go and not invest time in becoming anxious and depressed

- *Unrealistic high standards*: we can condemn ourselves for making a mistake or rebuke ourselves for an action when we would have preferred to have acted differently. We need to accept our strengths and limitations and realise that it is simply not possible to get everything right all the time

- *Double standards*: we can expect more from ourselves than we would from another person, and as a result we can be very hard on ourselves. We need to learn to treat ourselves as fairly as we would another person

- *Assuming powerlessness*: pessimism about the chances of things changing is central to depression. We can give up before we even start or we can allow events in the world at large to feed our depression. We need to make an effort to try to change our situation, as inaction only feeds our depression. As regards worldwide issues and problems – reality is the way it is, so we need to accept what we cannot change or try to address issues in whatever small way we can

- *Predictions of or speculations about the future and people's thinking*: a negative outlook can very quickly provoke depression. Being immersed in our negative predictions of the future means we cut ourselves off from the chance of change by not being open to alternative possibilities, which is essentially where most of our solutions lie. With negative speculations about what other people are thinking, we tend to put ourselves down and potentially harm otherwise positive relationships

A good method of challenging and testing your predictions is by stating your prediction clearly, and looking for existing evidence to either support or contradict it.

> *It's pointless. I can see no way out of this darkness. Why me? Why is everyone else so happy and yet, for me, the contemplation of death has become my best friend that visits me every day? There must be something very wrong with me.*
>
> *I can't control or change these horrendous feelings, so I must be inadequate in some way. Things have always gone wrong for me. Nothing goes right. Everyone will eventually leave. The future looks so bleak.*
>
> *Okay, I do have a few friends, but they are only around me because I have a car and money. Actually, they didn't ring me to go to the cinema yesterday, so that must be the beginning of the end. People are so selfish. They just take what they want and they don't care how you feel. I'm on my own again.*
>
> *Things should be better. I shouldn't have this racing mind, and I should be able to control how I feel. I am obviously weak if everyone else can feel good but I can't. What is wrong with me?*

Major and Minor Stressors

Below is a list of major and minor stressors that can trigger a depressive episode. They are obviously different for every individual but even the smallest irritant or stressor can have a cumulative effect which can eventually result in depression. The stressors may not change, but by being able to identify the trigger and recognise the amount of stress that we encounter, we may be able to change our ability to cope.

Major stressors include:

- *Physical stressors* such as not getting enough sleep or working long hours
- *Emotional stressors* such as betrayal, anger, grief, guilt or worry
- *Social stressors* such as arguing, feeling isolated or giving a speech
- *Disease stressors* such as suffering from AIDS or cancer
- *Pain stressors* from a new or old accident or disease
- *Family stressors* such as divorce, birth or coping with age-ing relatives
- *Environmental stressors* such as noise from road works, the winter cold or smoke-filled rooms
- *Decision stressors* – where there are too many significant decisions to be made at home or at work
- *Commuting stressors* – in rush hour traffic or waiting for transport that doesn't arrive
- *Change stressors* such as moving home or leaving a job
- *Chemical stressors* such as nicotine, caffeine or a bad diet
- *Phobic stressors* such as exaggerated fears of animals, peo-ple, places or things
- *Work stressors* such as bullying, working long hours, job interviews, job security, lack of progression, etc.

Minor stressors include:

- Waiting for a phone call or for someone to arrive
- Losing a game (yourself or your favourite team)
- People who drive with their fog lights on
- Working with incompetent people
- Not being able to find something
- Queuing
- Being late or late cancellations
- Someone telling you what to do
- Being taken for granted
- A friend asking too much of you
- No hot water
- Anniversary of the death of a loved one
- Being treated like a child
- Feeling sick
- Dealing with bureaucracy
- Losing a phone number
- A spouse or friend being under stress
- Being told how you feel
- A machine not working

Negative behaviour, cognitive distortions, major stressors and minor irritants can all build up inside us until they become too much and result in unhealthy consequences such as anger, anxiety, arguments, withdrawal or depression.

We can try to shelve our irrational thinking and our small concerns but these issues can balloon into bigger problems which can then be brought to a climax by something trivial and unrelated. We can then dump our enlarged uncomfortable emotions on someone close to us or pick fights in a vain attempt to let go of our frustrating feelings. This not only upsets people around us but also eventually leads us to feeling isolated, disappointed and depressed.

We need to become very aware of how our behaviour, irrational thinking and various stressors can feed our negative emotions, and how challenging and changing them can also help. As depressives, we do not have the luxury of shelving our issues; it is important that we learn to deal with all our issues as they come up, before they mutate into depression-feeding behaviours.

Summary

- All our actions result in consequences that we have to live with

- Certain behaviours and inactivity will feed our depression, so it is important to make an effort to help ourselves

- Negative thinking and negative self-talk will feed our depression

- Cognitive distortions are ways in which we negatively manipulate the facts and reality of what we experience in life – a significant factor in how we feed our depression

- By being able to identify our major and minor stressors in life, we may then be able to adapt our coping skills and manage our depression in a more effective manner

4

Tackling Depression

Treatment Options

There are two main approaches to the treatment of depression: the medical model and the person-focused model. The medical model treats people with medication, and a course of anti-depressant tablets is usually prescribed over varying lengths of time. The person-focused model concentrates on psychotherapy and on the numerous activities that a person can undertake in order to improve their condition. It's an attempt to help a person find solutions to their own problems.

As a counselling psychologist, I very much believe in the person-focused model (also called the social model, as opposed to the medical model, which involves the use of medication). However, there are times when medication is a viable option. If you are experiencing mania (see Chapter 1) or a psychosis, which is a severe mental derangement, then medication may be a necessary option in order for you to function properly in everyday life. Others have felt so stuck in the darkness of depression that they have also turned to medication to help them. If this is an avenue that you wish or need to go down, then you should contact your local GP. Your GP can be a good place to start as he or she may have to give you a letter of referral to a suitable psychiatrist for your needs.

The majority of people do not want to take prescription medication, and there are many who report dependence on the tablets and significant difficulties when trying to come off them. If a person has these concerns, I would recommend a course of psychotherapy; however, advice on medication must be sought from a doctor or psychiatrist. Most people report not being able to lift themselves out of depression on their own and a course of treatment with a competent therapist is perhaps the best way to begin to learn to manage depression. I strongly believe that if you are on medication you should also see a therapist, as a pill alone does not help you to learn how to manage your life.

The length of time you need to spend in therapy depends on the issues you have to deal with. Books can help you to identify your problems and ways to begin to tackle your depression. However, therapy can help significantly by releasing depressed emotions, by challenging ourselves in ways that we may wish to avoid and by identifying behaviours that need to be changed. Counselling psychologists, psychotherapists and counsellors can all be helpful, but do check their qualifications, their accreditations and if depression is an area in which they work.

Steps Out of the Darkness

Different therapists will have different approaches to the treatment of depression. My own particular approach involves four clear and distinct steps. An individual may get stuck at any particular stage and because things are constantly changing it can be perfectly natural to discover new difficulties in a previously covered stage in the process. This approach tries to keep it as simple as possible, and a return to a previous stage may help to unblock an emotional impasse and give way to a lighter feeling. Movement between the steps may be necessary for an individual to be able to recognise an emotional obstacle that was previously hard to see. Basically, everyone is unique and everybody has their own distinct path to follow. There is no right or wrong; there is only the best method of recovery that works for you at any particular time.

1. *Identify and accept*: this is an essential first step because without an acceptance of how you feel there is nothing to change. At this stage you realise that depression is more than just sadness. This is an acceptance of your emotional state and an acknowledgement that you may need help of some sort in learning how to manage your life. The key issue at this stage is identifying your depression, and the acceptance of this reality usually brings the realisation that you can't deal with it on your own. There can be huge resistance to this initial step as it is not easy to accept your depression. It is important to remember that having depression is not a defect. It requires great strength of character to identify depression and even greater strength to accept it.

2. *Stop feeding the depression*: as we saw in Chapter 3, there are many ways in which we can feed our depression through our actions, inactions, thoughts and self-talk. It is vital to identify these processes, as any further work on trying to manage the depression will only be in vain if you continue to support the depression. The depression-feeding behaviours can appear obvious when we read them in a book, but sometimes what is sitting right

under our nose is often the hardest to see. Many people also disregard the simple-sounding procedures as being too easy as to have any effect. Very often what can appear simple can be quite difficult to achieve. Also, these simple procedures are often the most effective when trying to mange a more contented and balanced life. This stage may be returned to frequently by many, as behaviours are often ingrained in our characters and therefore are the most difficult to see, accept and change.

3. *Tackling depression*: this stage is about making an effort to address your depression. As this chapter will highlight, there are many useful methods that a person can undertake, and it is about experimenting with different activities and seeing what fits for you at any particular time. What doesn't work at one time may work at a later stage, so it is important not to completely disregard any of the ideas. There are certain core activities that can help the majority of people and these include exercise, filling your time and making an effort to find what works best for you as an individual at any particular time. It is about finding a balance in yourself and seeing what combination of ideas works best in the management of your depression.

4. *Keep up the good work*: this final stage concerns the maintenance of the work that you have already done and it involves the continued support of yourself. It is very important to remain ever vigilant as regards the consequences of your behaviour, and a regular assessment of self is crucial in maintaining the more contented life balance that has been achieved. As everything in life changes, so also may this life balance need regular adjustments. It is therefore of the utmost importance

that you remain open to adjustment and change when necessary. Many people falsely believe that the work is over when a more contented balance is achieved. This belief tends to add fuel to a natural depressive dip, with these individuals experiencing a devastating fall and a belief that they are back at the beginning again. It is perfectly natural to experience a drop in mood, and when this is accepted and adjustments are made, it can then become a much more manageable affair. Processes for the continued management of depression are expressed throughout this book and will be discussed in more detail in Chapter 9.

Steps Out of the Darkness

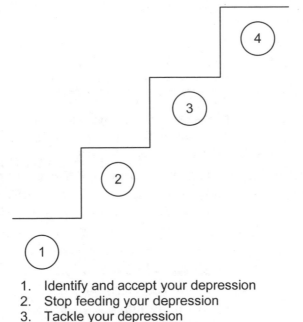

1. Identify and accept your depression
2. Stop feeding your depression
3. Tackle your depression
4. Keep up the good work

Effort and Energy

The biggest obstacle in tackling depression is finding the energy to make any changes. This energy can be hard to kick-start. However, as mentioned, the reality of most of our situations is that we probably need to make the initial effort in order to feel an increase in energy.

To do a minor job, or even to stand up and talk, can feel like it requires a phenomenal amount of energy, and in our darkest hours any effort can feel utterly impossible. We can see no benefit in engaging in any activity, and we foolishly believe that our only relief can be gained from remaining practically motionless.

Our depression seems to tell us exactly what to do in order for it to flourish. For example, our depression tells us to stay in bed, to stay in the house, not to talk; basically, not to involve ourselves in life at all. This lack of activity is paramount in feeding our depression, and it needs to be challenged by ourselves. We don't like to hear it but we need to accept it: we need to make an effort.

There are many people who don't understand what it is like to feel the hopelessness of depression. These are the people who tell us to 'Snap out of it' or, 'Sure, what have you to be depressed about?' and these are the people who we might feel like hitting. I suppose it's interesting that they can inject some sort of energy into us, but they have no understanding of what we are suffering. If it was as easy as they claim then I'm sure depression would probably not exist. However, there is an irony here. A solution can be as easy as making an effort in life, but making an effort can seem like an extremely hard endeavour.

We need to accept that whatever we are doing or not doing in life is actually not working. We need to try new ways and to experiment with new behaviours. It is about trial and error; building on what works, but being careful not to discard anything that doesn't as it may work at another time.

We need to be careful about feeling sorry for ourselves and doing nothing in our false belief that all is hopeless. Dealing with depression is about making an effort in life; it is about finding the right balance between mind, body and soul; it is about finding a new and more content way in which to live.

We get out of life whatever we put into it, so our lives can become even more empty when we do nothing. Making an effort is not guaranteed to make you feel better, but it can help to increase your energy and eventually you may stumble across something that could give you pleasure. Many will report that making an effort at least helps their depression to stabilise somewhat, and it helps them not to slide further into depression.

We all have had experiences of this in our own lives. The day we listened to our depression and stayed in bed under the duvet was the day we were climbing the walls by 11:00 a.m. and struggling with an escalating depression. However, the day we had to get up and do something was the day we didn't exactly feel better, but we definitely didn't feel any worse.

It is hard to remember anything positive when we are depressed. But, with practice, we can remember more readily the days when our depression lifted or even when it didn't take hold. The efforts that we made on these days may work again, or they may need to be changed to accommodate the different situations in which we find ourselves. The efforts that we make need to be recognised and commended as significant steps in helping ourselves.

It's 2:00 p.m. and I don't feel as bad as I usually do. The thought of getting up early today really upset me last night, but I am not as tired and weary as I had predicted. I actually have more energy than I have had in a long time, and I even shocked myself earlier with the thought of cleaning my room, doing a clothes wash and going to watch a match; it's a nice day.

When I think about it I don't know why I am so surprised, this happens every week. It's dole day, so I have to collect my unemployment benefit and do my shopping for the week. Every week I dread getting out of bed before 9:00 a.m., yet every week I rise without effort, and every week I feel the benefit of actually doing something with my day.

I know sleeping late depletes my energy and feeds my depression. I know that activity and even a small sense of accomplishment helps me to feel better, and I know that making an effort has a positive chain reaction.

It's hard to discipline myself when I have nothing to do, but I know that I need to continue this activity. I'll make the same promises to myself today that I make every time I feel enthused by my behaviour. I wonder if I'll make the change tomorrow, or just fall back into my passive existence.

Methods

Different models of treating depression were discussed earlier in this chapter, but the main focus of this book is on the practical procedures by which a person can help themselves. There are many ways of tackling depression, with each individual finding their own combination of techniques at any given time. Below is a list of the more common methods that have worked for people. It is not an exhaustive list, and I would encourage individuals to be creative in finding what best suits them.

Exercising

This is perhaps the most important effort that we need to make on a very regular basis, even when we are feeling well. Elite athletes have a lower incidence of depression than the general population, and this is thought to be related to the endorphin release through exercise. Exercise can also calm a racing mind, and help us to think more rationally and subsequently feel more content. Exercise may consist of a rigorous workout, a brisk walk or even doing a bit of gardening.

Filling Your Time

Many people can experience bad moods at particular periods in an average day or week; therefore, if you could identify such periods you would be in a position to make plans to fill such periods with activities, which could help to reduce opportunities for feeding your depression.

For example, through my work, I have come across people who dread Sundays for various reasons, and the thought of the day approaching would trigger negative thoughts and subsequent depression. However, when these people made the day their own and filled it with enjoyable activities, this had a positive effect. In some cases, it led to a significant improvement in their depression.

Effective time management can also be hugely beneficial in coping with depression and in relation to our self-esteem, our relationships with others and our work–life balance. Taking control of our time will afford us more control in our lives. Suggestions to assist in this endeavour will be dealt with in Chapter 9.

Mind, Body and Pleasure Balance

Happiness relies on paying attention to both our mind and body in our day-to-day life. People tend to get energised and revitalised by exercising their minds and bodies, and by engaging in various pleasurable activities. Depressed people can often identify a lack of balance between the mind and body in their lives. Too much of one thing can produce negative results. Balance is needed; the form that balance takes is different for each of us and what works for us will vary at different periods of our lives.

We must first identify our needs and then create an environment that helps us to meet them, without overdosing on one aspect and upsetting the entire balance.

> If all the year were playing holidays; To sport would be as tedious as to work.
>
> Shakespeare, *Henry IV*

Spirituality

For some people, a strong faith can be a great comfort and help in times of depression. For others, spirituality is something completely different. It could be philosophising on the great mysteries of life, marvelling at the mighty Atlantic swells or pondering the spectacle and vastness of a night sky. Paying attention to your spirituality can mean spending time in a place where you can feel most at ease and at peace with the world. The *Oxford English Dictionary* defines spirit as the animating or vital principle of man, and many find that experiencing nature or something bigger than ourselves can be very stimulating, empowering and calming.

Changing Routines

Although we can take great comfort from many of our routines, a change can have an invigorating effect on one's life. Even a slight change in our timetable can make room for another activity or can help us to appreciate an activity that we may have taken for granted.

Trying to Talk to People

It can feel like a gigantic effort to communicate with people, to concentrate on what they are saying and to understand their thoughts. We can isolate ourselves a lot when we are depressed, and we can become too obsessed with our own feelings, problems and thoughts; this is not healthy.

The irony is that we can find the solution for many of our problems in the words of other people. Although depressed people can have little interest in anything or anyone else, many report a lift in their energy and level of interest in life when they have made the effort to talk to people with similar interests or positive energy.

Planning Ahead

Upcoming events or occasions can cause anxiety or depression, especially when you are not prepared. For instance, it could be very helpful to prepare for an upcoming job interview or to study for an exam. Developing appropriate plans and coping skills to deal with risky situations will reduce depression and anxiety.

It may also help with your depression to have some sort of life-plan outline as regards career, the environment in which you want to live, personal development, and relationships and hobbies. It helps to review these plans regularly and to adjust them where appropriate.

Writing

It can be very frustrating to have one unfinished thought in your mind, and, just as you think you may be reaching a solution, to jump to another thought. This process can continue until you have many unfinished thoughts, and are much more frustrated than when you first began.

Writing can help to close and finish our thoughts; it can give us clarity, a different perspective on our dilemma, and it can help to de-clutter our minds. This, in turn, can prevent us from feeding our depression. However, when writing out thoughts, it is very important to finish the thought and not to leave the writing until we at least have a full stop on where our thinking has got to. Otherwise, the thought will remain unfinished and open, with the potential to feed our depression.

Writing a journal can also help with identifying efforts that have worked, or in dark times remembering periods that were more positive. You may also want to take stock of your recovery, so writing your own progress notes could be of great assistance. Ideas could include marking your depression at regular intervals on a one-to-ten rating scale, while also identifying areas needing improvement, and goals and target dates relating to these.

Decision Making and Problem Solving

Difficulty making decisions can be a part of most people's depression, and it is a significant factor in continuing to feed our depression. We can get overwhelmed with information, there can be much internal conflict in trying to find the best option, and the consequence of not making a decision may be to become depressed.

Common barriers to solving problems are:

- Not looking at all the evidence
- A reluctance to abandon an initial hypothesis
- Ignoring negative and absent information
- Probability can be ignored in preference for what is most common

Some techniques to improve our decision-making and problem-solving skills are:

- Using familiar objects in creative and useful ways
- Doing a 'pros and cons' list
- Putting the problem aside for a while so that a solution may occur to you (incubation)
- Breaking the problem into smaller elements and working backwards from the final goal (decomposition)
- Imitating the experts

Values and Beliefs

Identifying our highest values and beliefs can be of great benefit. When we act in ways which oppose our principles, inner conflict can occur, which in turn leads to depression. Our hypocritical behaviour often makes us depressed, but when we can match our behaviour with our values then we can often feel better.

From another perspective, our belief and value system can also put pressure on us in that we can acknowledge our worth by how other people react to us or by the quality of our work. This is guaranteed to lead to depression as our feelings are then subject to good and bad days, and other people's moods. It is important that we live life for ourselves and that we don't rate ourselves on our work or on what we think others might think of us.

Awareness of Consequences

We need to become aware of the consequences of our behaviour, and adapt and change our activities so as to produce the positive consequences, and hence more contented feelings. It is a matter of becoming aware of what motivates us, or increasing our self-awareness of our internal and external emotional triggers and the feelings and behaviours that they elicit.

Although many report that this awareness can be difficult to attain, one way of achieving it is to compare and contrast how we felt on different days as a result of different thoughts about ourselves, emotions or particular situations and events. This can be a process of isolating, identifying and eliminating unhealthy behaviour patterns; it is a process of trial and error. Remember not to completely disregard any behaviour as it may work on a different occasion.

We need to be creative in this endeavour and try activities that we think wouldn't even interest us. We need to think outside the box and experiment with new behaviours. It is worth the effort as we may just stumble upon something that could give us great pleasure and relief.

Design a Treatment Plan

A treatment plan involves identifying supportive behaviours and structuring the day and week with relevant activities that will stimulate our energy and help us to manage our depressions. This plan needs constant evaluation and adjustment, if necessary, but most importantly it needs to be strictly adhered to.

Our plan may not always produce immediate benefits, and in good times we may be tempted to take our foot off the pedal; however, letting go of what works for us can ultimately feed our depression. A break can be very beneficial, but if we stop making an effort in our lives, it is very likely that our depression will return.

Goals and Lists

It may also be helpful to identify short-term and long-term goals, as to have a purpose in life can be very effective in dealing with depression. Professional, social, financial, educational, intellectual, physical, spiritual, emotional or personal goals can not only give us something worthwhile to aim for, but they can also fill our time and provide welcome distractions from our depression.

Goals need to be specific and concrete, realistic and manageable; they are best broken into smaller, more manageable steps, with a sensible timeframe in which to achieve them. Likewise with a to-do list: it is best to make a small and achievable list that can be built upon gradually.

The setting of unachievable goals and making lists that are too big will have the effect of reducing motivation and increasing depression.

It's amazing how different I feel now compared to half an hour ago. I could feel myself falling fast into the dark abyss – I didn't plan this bank holiday, a beautiful day, and I had nothing to do. I am a strong believer in being active and involved in life and yet here I was again, motionless and staring at some crap on the TV. It felt like such a waste; I was beginning to get more and more anxious in my ever-increasing depression.

I jumped to my feet, turned off the mind-numbing TV, grabbed my journal and I looked back on what had worked before. This was an exertion, but my energy returned quickly as I began to write about my emotions and then identify future goals and plans. I was careful to finish my thoughts on paper and with each full stop came a great relief. I know what I need to do for myself, but writing about it just made it clearer and more obvious that I have the power to change my day and subsequently my mood.

With an idea fresh in my mind – and without thinking about it too much – I picked up the phone and rang my friend. We had a great chat, and I am now on my way to meet him to go for a walk by the sea. I am amazed at the difference that small effort made to my seemingly catastrophic mood. I feel hopeful again.

Coping Skills

As stated earlier, there are many approaches that can be used to alter our moods. Below is a list of methods used by people when managing their depression. Some of these are very simple.

- Do nice things for yourself: have a bath, listen to your favourite music, go to the pictures, read a book or a magazine, etc.

- Don't over think! When we wake in the mornings, we can sometimes think and worry about our depression so much that we are wrapped in darkness before our feet have touched the floor. Get out of bed quickly, get active and distract yourself, and by doing this the depression sometimes doesn't take as strong a hold as it would otherwise

- Identify problem areas in your work, personal or social life. Try to solve them, look for alternative options, accept them if they can't be changed or seek help

- Recognise the wisdom and potential coping skills that lie within many old mottos. For instance: 'Time flies when you're having fun', 'Look before you leap', 'No one is an island', 'One day at a time'

- Humour and laughter elicit a natural healing response from our bodies; endorphins are released which decrease pain sensation and perception, our mood is raised and our thinking becomes clearer. Look at the funny side of events, recall memories of laughter with friends or in films, or try to identify a humorous response to a difficult situation

- Make decisions about how to spend your time. Define your roles in your family life and personal life

- Money management is an area that is often avoided and can contribute to our depression. If money is a problem that will not go away, confront it and tackle it. It may cease to be a problem and thus stop feeding our depression

- Spending time by ourselves without feeling lonely can be essential to a healthy life balance. Solitude gives us time to reflect, and it gives us space away from everyday worries and responsibilities. It may be a skill that needs to be learned and nurtured, but it can be of great assistance in replenishing our depleted and lost energy and motivation

- Seeking solitude or comfort can be a very valuable coping mechanism when we are depressed. Finding a safe 'place' to retreat to can manifest itself as being the healing company of a particular person who you trust, as well as being a physical or emotional place. It could be a memory from the past that was warm and assuring; it could be a colour, a smell, a teddy bear, a pet or even a cuddly blanket

- Have something to look forward to, like a holiday, a meal out, meeting with friends, engaging in a hobby, etc. This can be a huge support during dark times

- Organising your home and work environments can facilitate feeling more in control, and a cleaner environment can also alleviate depressive feelings

- When depressed we can isolate ourselves from other people, but by keeping communication lines open with family and friends support can still be there when we are able to engage with it again. It is also helpful to evaluate all relationships and try to build on those that energise you, while letting go of the relationships that are draining

- Take risks in life, especially when the consequences and outcomes of success will be of a positive nature

- Avail of support groups

- Rewarding ourselves can help us to feel vitalised, which is essential in helping us to continue to perform our everyday functions. Give yourself a present

- We often deflect a compliment on our behaviour by belittling our actions in some way, and thus negating the compliment altogether. By just saying thank you and accepting the compliment graciously, we can learn to let the positive in and affirm ourselves. This will contribute to a healthy self-image and self-esteem

- By noting what is positive in others and communicating it to those that matter, we can learn to become more comfortable and used to a more optimistic outlook on life. Focusing on strengths rather than weaknesses will improve relationships and will enhance our own everyday functioning

- Improve communication and social skills by practising listening, sharing and questioning, which are all important social skills that help improve relationships

- Assertiveness and anger management are very important parts of coping with depression and these will be dealt with in Chapter 6

- As noted in the previous chapter (Chapter 3), ignoring or shelving small issues can lead to big issues which can eventually result in depression. No matter how small the issue, it therefore helps to address and deal with all issues as they arise

- A healthy balanced diet is recommended by many as essential in the management of depression

- Reading is a great comfort to many and a welcome distraction from negative and intrusive thoughts

- Various types of yoga, massage or other physical therapies can all be explored to see if they can work for you at any given time. This could also include fresh-air breaks, primal screaming or your own form of stretching. Be creative and explore the huge potential of alternative therapies

Essentially, tackling depression is about making an effort; it is about trial and error. It is also about learning to see the world differently, a technique that will be dealt with in the next chapter.

Summary

- Our depression will encourage us to feed it through inactivity; it is essential for us to make an effort in order to learn to manage our depression and feel better

- There are many methods for tackling your depression and creativity is encouraged in order to find what best suits yourself

- These methods of coping may require changing as different combinations will work at different times

- Making an effort usually increases the energy that we feel

5

Tackling Negative Thinking through Cognitive Therapy

The Link between Thought and Emotion

The link between what we think and how we perceive reality has a huge influence on our emotions. If I tell you something often enough, you will begin to believe it. If you tell me something often enough, I too will begin to believe it. However, if we tell ourselves something often enough, we start to believe it even quicker. As independent minded and as strong willed as we think we might be, we are, as humans, very open to suggestion and influence from others. Through psychological processes such as conditioning or reinforcement, humans can get orientated in certain directions, and our thoughts, beliefs and emotions can be influenced and sometimes even moulded.

This is very apparent all around us. The different cultures and environments into which we are born have a huge influence on how we see and interact with the world. Some psychologists used to postulate that by the age of three they could condition a child to be (in the future) a lawyer, a beggar or a thief purely through positive and negative reinforcement of relevant behaviour.

This process of repetition and the stimulation of our imaginations are very powerful tools of advertising. Look at the importance that we can place on clothes labels, different car manufacturers, the type of washing powder that we buy or even the soft drink that we might prefer. Do you think that it would all matter as much if we weren't constantly receiving subtle suggestions of the promise of happiness every time we turned the television on, or around every corner that we turned?

We are relentlessly being bombarded with messages of fear or promises of pleasure and bliss and, as a result, we all, at some time, believe that our contentment lies in the acquisition or consumption of items or, significantly, 'goods' – a word which we might associate with some inherent benefit.

There is no doubt that certain items can provide pleasure or reduce anxiety; this, however, is only transitory. We quickly become accustomed and bored, and then require further stimulation, which the manufacturers and service providers thrive on. It becomes a vicious circle, where true contentment is held in front of us like a carrot but can never actually be grasped. Most of us know this, but we are still susceptible to their empty promises; we are still prone to believe something when we hear it often enough.

However, as mentioned, what we tell ourselves is even more convincing than what others or society tells us. We can be tremendously unaware of how much and how often we speak to ourselves. However, in terms of depression or anxiety, this is very significant.

Most of us continuously chat away to ourselves, but it is the content of this dialogue that can have very negative consequences. Depressives tend to look at the world through very pessimistic glasses, and this is particularly significant in feeding depression (see Chapter 3).

If my thought patterns lean towards the negative and dark, as I begin to believe what I am telling myself my mood and emotions will reflect this. Thus, by my action of contemplating despair, I will become depressed as a consequence. If I think negatively, I will eventually become depressed. Therefore, sometimes being depressed is a choice, i.e. I would like to feel depressed so therefore I will immerse myself in negative thinking.

I'm unsure how I feel today; I had better get up now or I might fall back asleep and be late for work. The boss can turn nasty when he wants to, even if it's not my fault; he is so unfair and offensive when he does that.

I can just imagine if circumstances beyond my control, like an accident or a broken-down bus, made me late for work. He'd lose his reason, scream and shout at me, I wouldn't be able to get a word in edgeways, and he'd threaten me with dismissal. He'd accuse me of purposely being late and lying to cover myself; that is so ignorant, especially when I'm rarely late. He wouldn't listen to anything I had to say. He would shout over all my attempts to talk and he wouldn't believe me anyway. He is such an ogre.

At this point I suddenly come back to the present. I am only five minutes out of bed. I am brushing my teeth. I haven't even dressed myself and I am absolutely furious. I have done it to myself again; I wish I would stop winding myself up with exaggerated stories that haven't happened and probably never will.

> *My boss is actually quite reasonable; it's my imagina-*
> *tion that is the ogre.*

Cognitive Coping Skills

Cognitive therapy is basically about tackling our negative thinking and replacing our stressful thoughts with more encouraging inner dialogue. Cognitive distortions were discussed in Chapter 3, but here we will look at ways of changing these distortions into more realistic and ground-ed thoughts, and therefore into more positive feelings.

It must first be noted that negative thoughts will occur to us and this process is natural and out of our control. It is when we choose to entertain these thoughts for a period of time that we then suffer more from the resultant emotions. The process of mulling over these thoughts is in our con-trol, and it is this that needs to be challenged.

There are a number of ways by which we partake in upsetting ourselves, but the following three are what I see as the most common, and a good place to start before we look at tackling our negative thinking.

1. No Crystal Ball

We can spend a lot of time delving into the future, and if I predict negative outcomes then I will become depressed very quickly.

For instance, if I imagine a party I am going to next Sat-urday to be a disaster with no one wanting to talk to me, and that I will spend my time feeling humiliated by my iso-lation from everyone's company, I will quickly become depressed and probably won't go. But I don't have a crystal ball, and I can't tell the future; if I could I would be in the bookies making myself rich.

The party could be great; I could be the life and soul, meeting people with similar interests to me or even the person of my dreams. At the very worst, I can leave if I feel uncomfortable. We may also fear that we won't be able to communicate with others in social situations, but depressives will quite often surprise themselves at how well they can entertain with their incisive wit. When we ask ourselves what's the worst that can happen, we are often surprised at the outcome being a lot better than what we were imagining.

The consequence of this type of negative thinking is to become depressed. You have a choice: if you want to feel depressed, then by all means imagine some distressing outcomes in your future. If you don't want to become depressed, then let go of the crystal ball and try not to think of negative outcomes.

You can plan, but don't predict!

2. No Telepathy

Many of us can spend too much time worrying about what others think of us, so when this is mixed with a pessimistic outlook, we can have the potential to drive ourselves scatty. Depressives tend to focus on the negative and ignore any other possibilities.

For instance, if someone you know seemed to ignore you or grunt at you when you said hello to them the other day, if you are a depressive, you might have assumed that you had offended or upset that person in some way. If so, an internal dialogue of righteous anger may have ensued, with the consequence of you eventually feeling depressed.

The person may have had something on their mind and, although they seemed to see you, they could have being looking straight through you, totally preoccupied with their own thoughts. There are usually many other possibilities to explain other people's behaviour.

If, in a situation such as this, the other person matters to you, then ask them if everything is okay. You will most likely hear a positive reply but, on the off chance that you don't, at least you can either resolve the problem or begin the process of acceptance and moving on. Too many of us keep our concerns to ourselves with the consequence of depressing and upsetting ourselves as the issue continually arises for us.

We also consider ourselves far too important that other people would be thinking a lot about us; most people are more concerned about themselves. With this in mind, an embarrassing event is soon forgotten and turns into a funny story, and we will hopefully find that we are just like most people — thinking little of most situations and quick to move on.

3. Talk to Yourself Like You Would a Friend

Many of us are very hard on ourselves, putting ourselves down without mercy in situations where we would understand and forgive others. For instance, if a mistake is made, a depressive can tend to admonish themselves heavily, and believe that any attempt to succeed is a pointless endeavour; the consequence of this self-talk is to eventually feel depressed.

The language we use can be absolute, with plenty of 'always' and 'never', and this gives us the feeling of hopelessness and desperation. The truth is that sometimes we make mistakes and sometimes we get it right. Humans make mistakes, and that is just a fact of life that we have to get used to.

We should tell ourselves the truth and be as compassionate with ourselves as we are with others. The positive self-talk is best said out loud when possible, but it always needs to be talked fully through to ourselves; if we don't finish the positive thought , then we can still be left with the original feeling of depression.

These are the main processes involved in negative thinking, but there are many other subtle ways in which we can upset ourselves with our distorted thinking (see under the heading 'Cognitive Distortions' in Chapter 3 for a list).

The language that we use also has a significant effect on the creation of our moods. There is much meaning in many of the words that we use regularly, and most of us fail to notice the major input that these words have on our resultant moods. This may sound too simple to be of any use, but by changing our language we can radically change our emotions. Many of the following ideas have already been explored in Chapter 3, but they are of paramount importance in influencing our emotions, so another brief look from a different angle can only be of benefit.

A theme that runs through many of the cognitive tools to help you overcome depression is that you must remain in reality as much as possible. Depressives can be inclined to distort reality. Staying with the truth and looking at situations from all sides will significantly help when managing your depression. The following are examples of cognitive tools:

- *Don't use words like 'always' or 'never' when it is usually 'sometimes'.* These 'ultimatum' words will give the impression of an impossible situation and this will contribute significantly to feelings of hopelessness. Repeat the sentence by replacing the ultimatum word with 'sometimes' and note the difference in how you feel

- *Do not focus exclusively on the negative; look at the positive as well.* By focusing entirely on the negative you will develop a more pessimistic outlook on life and this will result in depression and feelings of hopelessness. For most of us, life is rarely exclusively negative, so looking at the reality that the positive also exists will significantly help to restore a more contented life balance

- *Don't jump to conclusions; stay with the facts.* A depressive's conclusions can very often be negative and, when too much thought is put into these falsehoods, the consequence is usually feelings of anguish and despair. (See sections under the headings 'No Crystal Ball' and 'No Telepathy' above)

- *Replace the words 'should' and 'ought' with a preference.* These words are overused by most of us, especially when talking to ourselves. They are judgemental and are often used as an angry response to something or someone. Self-talk of this kind will result in feelings of uselessness and dejection

- *Be careful not to magnify and exaggerate the negative, and not to minimise and disqualify the positive; stay with the truth.* As stated before, depressives can have a tendency to focus exclusively on the negative and exclude any other possibilities. It is important to stay with the truth of any situation, as this will most likely involve some positive aspects and will contribute to more contented emotions

- *Don't personalise events that have nothing to do with you.* Depressives can be predisposed to blaming themselves for things that have nothing to do with them at all. Try not to engage in this kind of thinking

- *Don't dwell too much on negative aspects of your past.* Although the past has happened, you need to accept that there is nothing you can do about it. Learn the lessons, but move on from these historical upsets as wallowing in them will cause you considerable distress and pain

- *Asking questions that have no answers will depress you.* Trying to achieve the impossible is a guaranteed way to depress and upset yourself

- *Be careful of unrealistic high standards; they will depress you if they are not achieved.* As stated above; the pursuit of the impossible will result in much anguish and torment

- *Be careful of double standards where you treat yourself more unfairly than you do others.* Depressives are particularly inclined to treat themselves in a much harsher fashion than if they were dealing with someone else. This unreasonable behaviour creates much distress

- *Develop a tolerance for ambiguity.* The only constant in life is change, so the search for certainties is really a search for the unattainable. There is much uncertainty in life and not accepting this will result in desperation and despondency

- *Change the things you can, but accept powerlessness when you can't.* Acceptance of this reality can have a major influence when dealing with depression. There are huge ironies in life and a major one is that by accepting powerlessness in appropriate situations, we can then become quite powerful individuals. Trying to change the unchangeable will result in frustration and grief. Acceptance of realities will help momentously in improving our negative moods

Negative thinking is sometimes referred to as 'stinking thinking' and there is a good story told to illustrate the consequences of such distorted thought patterns:

A man wanted to borrow a lawnmower from his neighbour. While on his way next door he suddenly remembered that he had forgotten to return a hammer that he had borrowed some time back.

'Oh, no,' he thought, 'I completely forgot. What will he be thinking, especially now that I want to borrow something else. He might think that I kept it on purpose, that I couldn't be bothered buying my own stuff, and that I'll just take his. How could he think this when we are such good mates and I genuinely forgot?'

The man was working himself up with his own anxiety and his distorted predictions, when he suddenly remembered that he had borrowed a rake and had also forgotten to return that.

'Dammit! He definitely now thinks that I am some sort of thief. How dare he! Especially when he knows me so well and I have been so good to him and his family. He has some cheek to judge me in such a way when it is a sincere mistake on my part.'

At that point the man had arrived at his neighbour's door, had rung the doorbell and was seething with anger. The neighbour opened the door, happy to see his friend, but was greeted by an angry finger being pointed at him.

> *'You have some cheek. To hell with you and your lawn-mower!' And the man stormed off.*

We can waste a huge amount of time thinking about situations that have not happened and never will happen. There is even more time wasted stewing in the resultant feelings.

The ideas above may sound quite simple but they are difficult to practise and they require a lot of effort before they can become effective coping skills. This is a very important area in which depressives need to challenge themselves.

Irrational Beliefs and Thoughts

It is not enough to challenge patterns of negative thinking; we must also identify and challenge irrational beliefs and thoughts. In Rational Emotive Behaviour Therapy (REBT), Albert Ellis postulates that we mainly feel the way we think. He proposes that all our uncomfortable feelings result from distorted beliefs and that, when these are identified and challenged, we can then change them into more rational thoughts and we will begin to feel better. The following are examples of irrational beliefs and irrational thoughts that can feed our negative thinking and our depression, and which need to be challenged in ourselves:

- I must have love and approval from all people that I find significant
- I must be thoroughly competent and making mistakes is unforgivable

- It is terrible when things go wrong
- My childhood will always affect me
- I must depend on others
- Healthy people don't get upset. I should always be happy
- People shouldn't act the way that they do, and they should be condemned for their wrongdoing
- The world ought to be fair
- I am not responsible for my behaviour or my problems, and I can't change how I feel
- I can do things only when I am in the mood
- I should be anxious and preoccupied by threatening situations
- Self-discipline is too hard and not needed to be happy
- I must always help others
- I must never show weakness
- Strong people don't ask for help
- I am inferior
- I need to be sure to decide
- Change is unnatural
- Working on my problems could hurt me
- Anxiety is always dangerous
- Willpower alone will solve all my problems

Distraction Technique

The distraction technique is simple but can be very effective in helping to combat intrusive negative thoughts. The main thrust of this technique is to distract ourselves from our negative thinking by concentrating our attention on something that is happening or existing outside of ourselves. Telling ourselves not to think about something will only cause us to dwell on that thought, perhaps leading to obsessive thinking. However, suggesting to ourselves that we concentrate on another issue, perhaps one outside ourselves, and some engagement with that will usually lead us away from negative self-statements. Below is a guideline, but be creative with these suggestions in order to find whatever works best for you.

Find a quiet place, close your eyes and focus on the worrying thoughts that were on your mind recently. This may increase anxiety, but that is to be expected. When the thoughts are clear, shout 'Stop!' either out loud or quietly to yourself, and then open your eyes. Immediately begin to describe all the objects that are in your line of sight and, being very detailed, describe all the characteristics of the items, from the colour to the shape to the size and the use of the item.

Watching television, talking to someone else, doing a puzzle, reading a book or even trying to read upside-down or through a mirror can all be useful methods of diverting your attention from what's bothering you. Be creative in finding ways to distract yourself and you will eventually find that your attention is drawn away from stressful thoughts and subsequently you will become more content.

Positive Experiences and Focus

Positive focus and a positive mental attitude can help us to combat negative thinking and it can protect us from negative feelings. Reflecting on positive past experiences or identifying ways to create similar ones can be very effective in coping with depression. Picturing these past experiences, remembering what they felt like and taking mental snapshots of these times can not only help at a particular moment but can also be revisited at other times.

We can be quite inexperienced at dwelling on positive memories or positive aspects of ourselves; so, again, practice is a key element of this coping strategy.

The following are examples of how you can focus on the positive:

- Remember something that you achieved or did well
- Look at positive relationships and friendships in your life
- Pick out one positive characteristic that you like about yourself
- Remember a time when you felt positive and proud of yourself
- Pick out a positive coping strategy of yours
- Note a way in which you can help yourself to stay positive
- Remember something positive that someone said about you
- Note a part of your life in which you feel positive
- Pick out a positive way in which you relate to others
- Remember times when you felt hope

Other ideas include writing positive statements down on a card and putting them in places where they will be read regularly. Also, if you memorise positive statements and associate them with certain objects in your home or elsewhere, simply looking at these objects can remind you of the positive statements.

Daily Record of Dysfunctional Thoughts

Using a written record of irrational thoughts and exploring more rational responses can help us to identify, address and change our behaviour more quickly for a better outcome. On the next page is an example of such a record, but I would encourage you to be creative in discovering what format or method is best for yourself.

The ideas explored in this chapter may all sound quite simple and therefore not effective, but research has shown cognitive therapy to be as effective, if not more, than drugs in the treatment of depression.

However, I would encourage you to not take my word for it, but to experiment with these exercises and to find out for yourself. Plenty of practice is needed as it can be quite difficult to change an engrained way of thinking. Every bit of effort will count.

Summary

- When we think negatively we tend to eventually believe these thoughts, and the consequence of this is that we feel depressed

- Negative thoughts will occur to us but by cutting short the time we spend in negative thought we can significantly affect how we feel

Record of Irrational Thoughts

Situation	Automatic Thought	Emotion	Rational Response	Outcome
Briefly describe the event	*Note the automatic thought that follows the emotion*	*Specify and rate the intensity of the emotion as a percentage*	*Note a rational response to the automatic thought*	*Specify and rate the intensity of the subsequent emotion as a percentage*
The boss gives out about something that wasn't done properly	I'm not good enough; I am going to be fired	Fear: 90% Worry: 80%	It's okay to make mistakes, especially when I am new. The boss gives out to everyone, but he does understand	Fear: 50% Worry: 40%
I got annoyed with the children	I'm a terrible father and a horrible person	Disappointment: 90% Shame: 80%	It's natural to get annoyed; writing myself off as a person won't help	Disappointment: 30% Shame: 50%

- Concentration on predicting positive rather than negative outcomes, and distraction and talking rationally to ourselves are the most important skills from which to start

- There are many more subtle ways in which we can upset ourselves and these include our irrational beliefs which, when challenged and changed, can help us to feel better

- A positive focus, reflecting on positive past experiences and positive aspects of ourselves, can help

6

Opening Up

Our Inner Selves

An essential part of dealing with depression is to look at our inner selves; otherwise it will be impossible to gain any awareness of how to manage our depression. Although no one knows what causes depression, everyone does know that it manifests itself because our emotions need attention. Therefore, we need to open up in order to begin the process of getting better.

Our early life experiences, significant and traumatic events in our past, family attachments and relationship difficulties, or distorted and inadequate coping mechanisms can all have a significant influence on our depression. Although the past is unchangeable, it may, however, be necessary for some of us to revisit parts of it in order to free ourselves in the present. It may also be that, by identifying old patterns of behaviour, we can only then choose to change our behaviour in the present.

Some of us can remain stuck with a traumatic episode or stuck with overwhelming emotions from the past. Some people need to relive these memories in order to gain freedom, while others can be free by just naming the emotions and subsequent effects. Different people have different ways of coping, but all coping requires some form of opening up. Even if some people decide not to address issues, to have come to this decision still requires some form of opening up and looking inside ourselves.

There is a practical side to dealing with depression that requires making an effort and filling our time, but there is also an emotional side that needs to be addressed. Much of our behaviour will need to be changed and before we can do this we will have to take a look at ourselves. One of the best coping mechanisms is to name our emotions and accept them, and to do this we will also have to take a good look inside ourselves.

Gender

Gender roles are behaviours, expectations and values regarded by society as being either masculine or feminine. They are embodied in the behaviour of men and women and are culturally regarded as appropriate to men and women. These values and beliefs are learned during early socialisation, when people first learn what behaviour is expected of them by society, and are based on rigid gender role stereotypes and beliefs about men and women (O'Neill, 1995). Gender role conflict is a psychological state in which socialised gender roles have negative consequences on the person or on others (O'Neill, 1982). Overall, gender role conflict implies cognitive, emotional, unconscious or behavioural problems caused by the socialised gender role learned in sexist and patriarchal societies (O'Neill, 1995).

Stereotypically, women are allowed all the emotions except for anger, while men are taught to only feel happy and angry. Women can be encouraged to seek help and support, while for men seeking help and expressing vulnerable emotions are deemed to be a sign of femininity and weakness and to be avoided at all costs. Although things can be less black and white than this, these traits do cause significant distress for people from early identification of depression to an eventual competent management of the problem. Denial of a problem, refusal to seek support, festering emotions and anger that gets turned inwards — these behaviours all cause considerable distress.

Stages of Opening Up

Although all stages of depression are fraught with negative emotions, there are certain stages that are common to all of us and these eventually require us to open up and look honestly inside ourselves.

Acceptance of the Problem

This is the first step in opening up and the first stumbling block that most people come across. To accept that you have a problem is for many people an acceptance that you are weak and flawed in some way. There can be huge resistance to this potentially earth-shattering realisation, and also huge resistance to believing that depression could actually affect us. It is usually the case that our depression gets so painful for ourselves and others that acceptance is the only possibility.

Seeking Support

One might think that once a person has accepted the problem then it may be easier to open up, but opening up can prove to be just as difficult if people become resistant to looking for help. Seeking support seems to take a deeper level of acceptance, perhaps a level from which there is no return, and this can excite fear. It is usually the case that once a person seeks support then they can feel a great sense of relief.

There are those who venture only as far as their local doctor and a prescription of anti-depressants; there are those who avoid the tablets and go into psychotherapy; and there are those who find support through both avenues.

As mentioned, my personal belief is that psychotherapy is an essential element in the treatment of all depressions. Tablets can help a person who is psychotic, manic or stuck in a very dark hole, but tablets on their own will not help a person to continue to manage their difficulties. I believe that all recovering depressives will praise the practice of opening up and looking inside oneself.

Psychotherapy

There is much fear and many connotations associated with the word 'psychotherapy'. Many Irish people associate psychotherapy with help for the clinically insane, or as being for those who are so ill that they can no longer function in everyday life. While psychiatry tends to deal with serious (as well as less serious) clinical conditions, psychotherapy is for people who function in daily life. The Irish are not as open about having a therapist as Americans can be, for instance, but therapists' rooms are full of your neighbours, your friends, your relatives and even your closest family members who keep this part of their lives a secret.

People are full of excuses as to why therapy wouldn't suit them but the truth seems to be that the thought of opening up and looking inside ourselves can bring up a lot of fear. Even when a person does eventually engage with therapy, it can take time for them to become ready to look at various parts of themselves. This seems to be the case for most of us, and psychotherapy tends to travel at the client's pace and in line with the client's progress.

Most people's experience of psychotherapy is of a very positive and life-changing journey. They find great relief in letting go of old stories, they find new coping skills of naming and accepting their feelings, and they come to see that looking inside themselves is an extremely beneficial process. Many regret not having done therapy years earlier.

Naming and Accepting Emotions

We discussed earlier (in Chapter 3) that we mainly feel according to the way we think, and we can feed, create and choose many of our feelings by how we think or talk to ourselves. It is also true that many of our feelings also just happen and we have no control over this process.

We can all feel happy, sad, upset and content, and sometimes these feelings just appear out of nowhere. Many of us spend much wasted time trying to change or avoid how we feel, but by trying to change the unchangeable or avoid the unavoidable all we do is create even more upset for ourselves.

All our emotions will change. We know that good moods will change but we often believe that our bad moods will last forever. None of our moods have ever lasted forever, so by fighting our emotions we only make it worse for our-selves. The trick is to name the emotion and accept its existence. If this is difficult for us, it can be useful to iden-tify how we are experiencing the emotion physically so that in the future a lump in our throat, for instance, or butter-flies in our stomach may help us to identify more quickly how we are feeling.

Allowing ourselves to experience and feel our emotions is perhaps the most powerful of all coping skills. It can sometimes be difficult to stay with our feelings, but with practice we can achieve this goal and begin the process of allowing our emotions to flow through us without them getting stuck or festering for long periods of time.

Watching a sad film or listening to emotive music may help us to cry or help us to stay with the feeling that needs to be expressed in order for it to be released.

I found it so hard to accept that there was anything wrong. Yes, I felt terrible; yes, I had lost interest in prac-tically everything; and, yes, I was isolating myself and just angry with the world at large. I believed that I could deal with anything that was thrown my way; if I could manage my family then I could manage anything.

In hindsight, I can see now that I was a wreck. I was so sensitive to any emotional trigger, I was walking a tightrope, bursting into anger or tears with the slightest of touches. I was so afraid to admit that there was some-thing wrong as I felt that my life would disintegrate, and also those lives that depended on mine. I can now see that by not accepting the reality of my situation, I ran a greater risk of our world coming apart.

My partner made me see myself clearly. There was much anger and tears; I was very resistant to accepting any vulnerability. It was unpleasant for both of us to say the least, and then I resisted seeking any form of help. Sure now that I knew I was depressed, wasn't that enough? And surely I could sort it out myself.

I finally acquiesced to going to the doctor, but psychotherapy was for the insane, and I was no 'loop the loop'. I was afraid. It took me a long time to see and accept this, but I was absolutely terrified of looking inside myself.

There was too much in there, but I found a therapist who I liked and trusted, and in time I began to deal with all my issues. The initial session was nerve-racking but a huge relief; I was finally going to let go of all my pain and stop experiencing the emotions that I was still carrying from my childhood and adolescent years.

Holding on to these emotions has caused me much distress throughout the years. Letting go has opened up a new existence for me that I never thought possible. I am less tense, I feel more stable; and by accepting that I am depressed, I can now manage my life much more effectively. I regret not doing therapy years earlier.

Many personal issues can and need to come up to be released; these are unique to each individual and dependent on his or her own life experiences. However there are a number of common issues for people when dealing with depression and these are discussed below.

Anger Management and Assertiveness

For a lot of us, anger can be an integral part of our depression, and managing it appropriately is vital for us to achieve any sense of relief. We get angry when we look for causes of our depression, trying to find an origin which we can fix and mend and therefore feel much better. This is a futile endeavour as it is very rare that there is only one simple cause or one simple issue that needs changing, so this effort tends to frustrate us even more.

We also get angry at the immoveable quality of our depression and the seeming pointlessness of this emotion. When this anger remains inside us, or it becomes a constant in our daily lives, we then run the risk of the anger affecting us physically in the form of stress-related illnesses such as ulcers or back pain.

Being able to name and accept how we are feeling is an essential coping skill needed to deal with life issues. Many people cover vulnerable emotions with anger and if we are unable to look underneath this shield to see how we are really feeling, we can then deny ourselves a means of reducing our depression. This is not only very damaging to our close relationships but also very destructive to ourselves.

Anger and frustration is a natural part of depression. When many of us believe that we are not supposed to express or even feel this emotion then the anger can turn inwards and can manifest itself as more damming self-statements or sometimes self-harm. Realising that it is acceptable to be angry and finding an appropriate way to express it is an indispensable coping skill.

Understanding Your Anger

Getting to know your anger is the first step. There can be *physical symptoms* such as a tense jaw, grinding teeth, neck or back pain, headache, dizziness, sweaty palms, clenched fists, red face, energy loss or rigid posture. There may be *emotional symptoms* such as guilt, resentment, anxiety, the feeling of wanting to run away or lash out, unease or embarrassment. There may also be *behavioural symptoms* such as screaming, sarcasm, abusive behaviour, getting into trouble, substance use or overeating. An anger diary in which we note our triggers, reactions and alternative responses may assist in getting to know our anger.

Some people can deny their anger by ignoring it or pushing it down, while others can allow it to build to an eventual explosion. It is important to know how long or short your fuse is so that when you are angry you know how long it takes for you to explode. It is also important to be very aware of the consequences of your anger.

Does your anger ...

- Lead to aggression?
- Harm your relationships?
- Contribute to physical problems?
- Compromise your mental health?
- Interfere with work, family or social life?
- Last too long and become too intense?
- Appear too frequently and flare up too quickly?
- Result in physical damage?
- Result in legal ramifications?
- Lead to self-harm?

Managing Your Anger

There are many suggestions as to how to manage your anger and deal with conflict resolution. They involve open, honest and direct expression, as well as physical and emotional techniques that can facilitate calmer expression and communication:

- Anger may need a physical release, so go for a run, do some press-ups, punch a bed or scream into a pillow. Tightening and releasing your muscles or imagining yourself screaming may help if you are not in a position to engage in a form of exercise

- Pick a good time to address the issue if another person is involved, i.e. not when you are hungry, furious or tired, and likewise for the other person

- Walk away for a time, if possible

- Remember your body language: maintain a respectful personal space, use a firm but not aggressive voice, and establish direct and level eye contact when possible

- Pick a neutral place for confrontation, away from people's homes, which are places of power

- Establish the needs of both parties

- Plan a discussion in advance; practise what you want to say

- Express yourself clearly and don't apologise for it

- Use short sentences that are direct and to the point

- Ask questions, do not assume

- Ask for what you want in a specific and direct manner

- Leave silences; don't fill them with unnecessary dialogue

- Don't drag in old issues

- Avoid tangents; use the broken record technique of repeating the question or statement so as to remain focused on the issue at hand

- Don't attack or blame the person. Begin your expression of emotion with 'I' statements; otherwise the person can feel accused and they will instinctively defend themselves

- Listen to and recognise what others have to say

- Learn to say no; practice will help

- Avoid absolute terms such as 'always' or 'never'. A person can react angrily to these unfair statements and your point can be lost in the heightened emotions

- Avoid vague and general statements; be specific

- Problem-solve; look for solutions and compromises

- Asking the other person for their opinion or for help is an effective way of problem solving

- Ask a third party to become involved

- Writing a letter to the person can help you to become clear in what it is that you want to say, or you may want to give it to them to avoid the unnecessary distractions of other emotions and issues

- Use relaxation techniques, or listen to calming music

- Be careful of negative self-talk; be positive and realistic with yourself

- Learn to accept positive feedback and criticism

- Learn to accept other people's points of view, and that people and situations - past, present and future - will not change. Change what you can but accept what you cannot change

- Restate the other person's concerns and opinions when disagreeing as it shows that you are listening and have respect for them
- Criticise the act not the person
- Learn to forgive, not only others, but also yourself
- Focus on the present
- Respect the other person's right to say no or to express how they feel

Remember that remaining angry will only eat ourselves up both physically and emotionally. It is important for a balanced, healthy lifestyle for us to identify a time limit in which to confront, address and move towards letting go of our anger.

Assertiveness

The above techniques can also be used to achieve assertiveness, which for some people is a crucial element in managing their depression. Before we look at the different types of assertiveness it is important to recognise our rights as a human being. These may be obvious to most of us, but it is surprising how many of us confuse and ignore our rights and as a result we can become depressed.

I have the right to:

- Make mistakes
- Change my mind
- Change a situation
- Be treated with respect

- Feel and express all emotions
- Say no without feeling guilty
- Say that I don't know, I don't agree and I don't understand
- Ask for what I want
- Recognise my own needs and wants independently of others
- Enjoy my successes
- Be imperfect
- Ask for help and have a support system
- Have privacy
- Respond and do things in my own time
- Determine my own priorities
- Set my own boundaries
- Express my opinions
- Decline responsibility for other people's problems
- Deal with others without being dependent on them for approval
- Be listened to and taken seriously
- Expect honesty from others
- Be myself
- Not assert myself

The above list can be expanded enormously. We may compromise ourselves by disregarding our own needs and living our lives in fear of what might happen or with concern for other people's reactions; this will most likely lead to depression.

Types of Assertiveness

- *Passive assertiveness* is allowing people to walk all over us while believing their rights to be more important than our own. These people avoid conflict, they are too accommodating, they want to be liked and they do not stand up for themselves

- *Aggressive assertiveness* is about getting our own way, and considering our own needs and wants as more important than anyone else's. These people are loud and pushy; they dominate and intimidate people, while violating other people's rights

- *Indirect assertiveness* is about getting your needs met by indirect means such as manipulation. Such assertiveness can be viewed as sly or under-handed

- *True assertiveness* is about recognising our own needs and that of others as being of equal importance. People with this quality give equal respect and consideration to their own needs and wants and those of others

An assertiveness diary could help you to evaluate your interactions with people on a daily basis and to become aware of your choices in terms of communication with them. The diary could detail situations, your responses and other's responses to them, your resultant feelings, and other possible assertive responses.

I felt like I was constantly hitting pillows. I could do nothing to change my situation; my sad emotions wouldn't go away and I felt that everyone was abusing my good nature. They were so selfish: I would go out of my way to help them and yet they would refuse if I needed a favour. People are so self-centred.

I am suffering here, I feel helpless, and although I do feel sad and vulnerable I am just furious with the world. The anger helps me to feel somewhat empowered, and if I don't express it in some form then I think I'll crack up. I am angry with most people around me; I never say no to them and they say it to me all the time. How self-centred can you get?

It took me a long time to see what I was doing. My anger was frustration which dissipated when I finally got some professional help and learned to express how I was really feeling. It was also linked to me being a doormat and allowing people to walk all over me. When I took responsibility for myself and learned to be assertive and say no, this changed my life and I began to have healthy relationships with the people around me.

I blamed everyone else, expecting them to change, but that is an impossible wish, and it was only when I changed myself that my world began to change and I began to feel much better.

Other Issues

Opening up is also essential for us to identify and deal with other issues in our lives that may be feeding our depressions. For instance, awareness of our *strengths* and *vulnerabilities* is crucial in identifying sensitive areas that may feed our depressions, and also in recognising our capacity to cope in our dark hours. Identifying and challenging our *value systems* can help hugely with negative thinking and forming more rational beliefs. Setting *personal boundaries* with people can increase our sense of control and self-esteem, and it can limit the depressive effects that we can let others have on us.

Other depression-feeding issues of concern to people relate to negative body image, relationships with family and friends, difficulties with parenting, addictions, bereavement, anxiety and stress, and so on.

The list is endless and unique to every individual, but the point is that, as we open up, identify and deal with our concerns, we can begin the process of learning to manage our depression.

Summary

- We need to look inside ourselves in order to learn how to manage our depression

- There are stages of opening up that are common to all of us and they are strongly linked with our acceptance of depression

- Anger management and assertiveness are shared themes for most of us when dealing with depression

- Understanding and addressing our level of assertiveness and our anger can help significantly in managing our depression

7

Suicide

A suicide often leaves relatives and friends bewildered by the mystery that surrounds the person's actions, shocked at the extreme violence that the person has inflicted on themselves and emotionally confused in trying to cope. Even if a person was very obviously depressed, it could still have been very difficult to predict whether they were about to take their own life.

We will first look at some facts and figures about suicide in Ireland and then at a brief history of suicide, and some theories and certain myths surrounding suicide. Warning signs and factors associated with suicide will be discussed in an attempt to partially explain why a person can undertake such a course of action. Ways to help someone who is suicidal, as well as coping with bereavement following suicide, will also be discussed.

Facts and Figures

The astounding number of people, particularly males, taking their own lives in Ireland is a major cause for concern. In 2003, there were 497 suicide-related deaths, with 87 of these recorded as undetermined, while in 2008 there were 424, with 181 undetermined (National Office for Suicide Prevention, 2008). More people have died from suicide between 1970 and 1995 (circa 6,000), than have been killed in the Troubles in the North (circa 3,000), and suicide has been accepted in Ireland as the principal cause of death in young people, exceeding accidents and cancer (McKeon, 1998). One in every 59 Irish deaths is by suicide, and the rate of suicide has exceeded that of road traffic accidents since 1997. It is estimated that, in the Republic of Ireland, 25 people try to take their own lives each day, while it has been estimated that up to 6,000 people attempt suicide each year in Ireland (Egan, 1997).

Worldwide, it is estimated that 2,500 people kill themselves each day, with 30 million people attempting suicide each year (Connolly, 1998). Dr Kelleher (1937–1998), who established the National Suicide Research Foundation in Ireland, estimated the cost to society at IRL£4 billion annually in Europe. It is also estimated that for every suicide there will be 43 people affected emotionally (Connolly, 1996). This suggests that suicide and its related effects have reached epidemic proportions.

The irony of the situation is that, while more people are dying from suicide, more money is being spent on the prevention of other causes of death; this, however, is not meant to suggest in any way that money be taken away from these causes. It must also be noted that the actual figure for deaths by suicide may be higher as there are legal restrictions on coroners declaring a death by suicide, and families sometimes conceal the real cause of death due to the stigma attached to suicide. The under-reporting of suicide deaths may also arise because there is no commonly accepted definition of suicide for data collection purposes.

The Psychological Society of Ireland (1992) describes suicide not as a disease but as an expression of a host of emotions - hopelessness, guilt, sorrow, loneliness, rage, fear, shame - that have roots in psychological, social, medical and biochemical factors. A definition is given by the World Health Organisation: 'Suicide is an act with a fatal outcome that is deliberately initiated and performed by the deceased him/her self, in the knowledge or expectation of its fatal outcome, the outcome being considered by the person as instrumental in bringing about desired changes in consciousness and/or social condition.'

The word 'suicide' comes from two Latin words: *sui* meaning self and *occidere* meaning to strike or to kill. In Irish, suicide is *féin mharbhú*, which means self-murder.

It must finally be noted that there are other forms of suicide, such as neglecting to have oneself treated for a physical disorder, continuing to indulge in behaviour that you know could lead to death or not taking necessary medicine; such deaths are seldom reported as suicide.

History

Throughout history, suicide has been both commended and condemned. The Roman philosopher Seneca praised it as 'the last act of a free human', while the Greeks permitted convicted criminals to take their own lives, as when Socrates drank his hemlock. In South-East Asia there is a tradition of self-sacrifice by way of social protest, and this has also been seen in the form of the hunger striker or suicide bomber. In Japan, *hara-kiri*, the ritual suicide by self-disembowelment on a sword, has been permitted and honoured, as was *kamikaze* – suicide attacks on enemies by Japanese military aviators in times of war. The Brahmas of

India also honoured the person who freed himself from his body, and they praised the widow who committed *suttee*, which was to throw herself on her husband's funeral pyre.

Suicide has also been viewed as altruism from a Darwinian perspective. This was the intentional killing of the self leading to the increased survival chances of the family or community. For example, among certain Inuit, suicide of an elderly and infirm person would be actively aided by a person's family, friends or community in times of severe food shortage.

The Jewish Talmud describes suicide as sinful. Islam certainly doesn't approve, with the Koran describing suicide as a crime graver than homicide. In the first centuries of Christianity many gave their lives in martyrdom; however, in the fourth century, St Augustine changed this thinking when he proclaimed suicide a crime because it violated the fifth commandment – 'Thou shalt not kill.'

In England until 1870, suicide was defined as an act of self-destruction while of unsound mind and was punished by the forfeiture of the deceased's estate to the crown. In some areas the survivors (those close to the person) had to pay a penalty as they were seen as accomplices and most survivors had to go to a place where they were not known (Nowlan, 1998).

The Catholic Church also prevented the body of a suicide victim from being buried in consecrated ground, or, if they were, they were pushed to the north wall of the graveyard. In Ireland, suicide remained a crime until 1993, while the Catholic Church now emphasises that suicide is a mortal sin only if committed with a clear mind.

Theories of Suicide

Many theories have been put forward to explain or to attempt to understand suicide. Freud suggested that suicide was originally a death instinct (Freud called the death instinct Thanatos), a force which works continuously towards death and was essentially an aggression which was turned inwards against the individual. Neurobiological theories suggest that suicide is partially heritable, with low serotonin and certain genes and receptors in the brain perhaps playing a role. Other studies have shown more suicides following media coverage of a celebrity suicide than after the death of a celebrity from natural causes.

Much psychological research points to the importance of early childhood experiences in the development of our personalities, in that these experiences determine in many ways how we deal with the problems of life in later years. Our security later in life may be determined by how much love, care and warmth we encounter as children. Related to this are developmental factors that look at the extent to which individuals have learned to act in particular ways in difficult circumstances.

Cognitive theories focus on the distorted thinking and irrational reasoning that many people report prior to a suicide attempt. This can be illustrated in the following passage, which may seem incredible to a rational thinking person in how someone can turn the absurd and irrational into the logical, realistic and irrefutable.

They'll be better off without me. I can see the worry and concern all over their faces: my wife is developing permanent lines on her forehead, while my kids are afraid to even look at me for fear of upsetting me. They tip-toe around me, they rarely ask me questions or even talk to me at all. There's no laughter in the house anymore; there's only tension and depression where once there was ease and contentment. It's all different now, it's not going to change and it's down to me.

I feel so separate from them and everybody; there's no interaction between me and my family and friends. I can hear the kids and my wife talking but it all stops suddenly when I enter the room. 'Are you alright, Daddy?' 'How are you doing today Love?' I can see how much I am upsetting them. I love them very much, so I have decided that this must stop now and they need to enjoy the rest of their lives.

They may feel sad for a time, they probably will, but it will pass and then things will be great. Their lives are affected by me too much, they mind me too much and I have begun to bring them down. What I have can obviously be contagious, so my decision will also protect them now and in their later life. I must protect them from this pain; there is no other way.

My brothers and sisters – who have seen me growing up – will understand; some of them suffer from depression themselves. Most of my friends who know me well will understand too. They'll all probably feel sad that it had to come to this, but they'll see that this is the best and only course of action. Things would never have changed. It is the only course of action and they will eventually commend me for my bravery. They won't have to worry about me again, contentment and laughter will return to their lives and I will finally be free from this incurable agony.

Myths about Suicide

- People who talk about suicide don't commit suicide

    - *Up to three-quarters of these people do*

- After a crisis, the suicide risk is over

    - *Many suicides occur in a period of improvement*

- Suicide happens without warning

    - *Indications are often given*

- Suicide occurs mainly among the rich/the poor

    - *Suicide occurs in all groups in society*

- People who attempt suicide by low-lethal methods are not serious about killing themselves

    - *Many people overestimate the lethality of certain methods or pill doses and therefore they make nonlethal attempts when they really want to die*

- Suicidal people want to be on their own

    - *Most suicidal people do not want to be on their own*

- Suicidal people are absolutely intent upon dying

    - *Many are ambivalent and may retain a desire to live*

- You are either the suicidal type or not

    - *It could happen to anyone*

- You have to be mentally ill to commit suicide

    - *Suicidal behaviour indicates deep unhappiness and despair, not necessarily mental illness*

- Once a person becomes suicidal, they are suicidal forever

  - *Suicidal thoughts may or may not ever return*

Warning Signs

The question that concerns all professionals and anyone who is worried about someone who they think could be contemplating suicide is how can they recognise that the person is seriously thinking of taking their own life.

Although it is estimated that up to three-quarters of all suicides give some warning, it can still be extremely difficult to predict whether someone will take their own life. If a person doesn't want you to know then it is virtually impossible to detect any such thoughts. However, there can be a number of warnings, and if any or a number of the following signs exist in a person at any particular time then the risk of suicide may be greater. It must also be noted that many people showing the following signs may never seriously contemplate suicide and these signs may not be an indication of a suicide attempt. A combination of certain characteristics and experiences may prompt a suicide attempt in a given person at a particular time under certain circumstances.

- Direct verbal warning or indirect reference
- Depression
- Hopelessness
- Reactive depression to an upsetting life event
- Resistance to an underlying depression
- A history of previous suicide attempts

- A history of suicide in the family
- Being single, divorced or separated
- Living alone; feeling isolated and lonely
- Unemployment
- Gender: in Ireland, men are up to four times more likely to commit suicide
- Age: in Ireland between 2002 and 2006 risk of suicide increased for males in their early twenties and for women in their early fifties (National Office for Suicide Prevention, 2008)
- High-risk behaviours, where mistakes or a lapse of concentration could result in death
- An anti-social personality and other mood disorders
- People with social difficulties and in social isolation
- Schizophrenia, especially in the early stages
- Impulsive behaviour – where people tend to act and react without taking the consequences into consideration
- Rigid thinking with little space for change or mistakes
- Having an eating disorder
- Alcoholism and drug addiction
- Intoxication: between a quarter and a third of all suicides involve people who have been drinking alcohol
- The suicide of a close relative or close friend
- Jokes, drawings or music about suicide
- Speaking of re-union with the deceased
- Being in prison

- Being overwhelmed by the disparity between expected achievement and actual accomplishments
- A recent humiliation
- Bereavement: a large percentage of people who commit suicide have experienced a family death within the last three years
- Being the child of abusive, rejecting or depressed parents
- Serious physical illness
- Serious personal crisis; current and anticipated
- Significant stress
- Withdrawal from relationships
- Poor problem-solving skills
- Release from hospitalisation: risk is greatest during leave from hospital or after discharge
- The break-up of a relationship or the death of a spouse or partner
- Unexpected and sudden reduction of performance at work, in studies or in family life
- Constantly dwelling on problems for which there seem to be no solutions
- Homosexuality
- Out-of-character behaviour, such as shoplifting
- Perfectionism
- Sudden and significant mood changes, emotional instability or becoming very content and serene having been quite depressed
- Loss of self-esteem; poor confidence

- Sleep disturbance, insomnia and/or early-morning waking
- Sense of helplessness about the future
- Financial stress
- Indirect statements and behaviours such as tying up loose ends, giving away personal items or emotional and definite goodbyes
- Sexual problems
- Deterioration in physical appearance and personal hygiene
- Depressive effects of prescription drugs
- Getting disproportionately upset over minor issues

Some of these signs are discussed in greater detail below.

Conditions and Circumstances Associated with Suicide

Psychiatric Disorders

Psychiatric illness has been consistently shown to be present in the majority of those who commit suicide. Studies in Ireland and abroad show a strong connection between mental illness and suicide, with over 90 per cent of suicide victims having been diagnosed as mentally ill. The most common disorders are alcohol dependence, major depression, anxiety disorders and social phobia. Other common disorders associated with suicide are avoidant and paranoid disorders, and borderline personality disorders, as well as people with learning disabilities.

Depression has been consistently shown as a condition in those who commit suicide, and it is believed that 15 per cent of people with recurring depression and bipolar disorder will kill themselves (Pallis et al., 1984). Schizophrenia has also a comparatively high association with suicide, occurring in over 10 per cent of suicides, with the majority of these believed to also suffer from depression. Frequent relapses and social isolation may also be indicators of suicide in schizophrenics.

A time of increased risk of suicide for psychiatric patients is the period immediately following discharge from psychiatric care. According to *Suicide in Ireland: A National Study* (Government of Ireland, 2001), almost a third (31.4 per cent) of those treated as psychiatric in-patients died within three months of being discharged from hospital. In general, the problem seems to lie in the inability to function adequately in society following a period in psychiatric care; however, many other factors may apply.

Physical Illness

Chronic physical disorders can be common among suicide victims, including those with conditions such as Huntington's disease, Parkinsonism and AIDS. This may be due to several factors, including pain, depression, alcohol abuse and difficulty coming to terms with a significant change in life circumstances.

Biochemical Abnormalities

While much research has shown that serotonin abnormalities can have a significant link to depression, they have also been linked to suicide. It has been shown that the breakdown products (the result of serotonin being broken down) of the neurotransmitter serotonin are lower in depressives with suicidal behaviour. This reduced serotonin turnover may be associated with a lower threshold for aggressive responses and also with impulsivity, and these associations may be the link with suicidal behaviour. Lower serotonin may also lead to a person isolating themselves, poorer problem solving and poorer judgement.

Genetics

Studies of suicide within families have shown that if suicide has occurred within a family the chances of it happening again within that family are increased. According to *Suicide in Ireland: A National Study*, 18.8 per cent of the sample surveyed had a family history of suicide or deliberate self-harm. Related to this may be the issue that parental depression not only contributes genetically to the development of mood disorders in offspring, but also to attachment and development difficulties. People from families with high levels of mental illness, alcoholism and low or no family support have been shown to be at increased risk of suicide.

Social Factors

The French sociologist Emile Durkheim postulated that substantial variation in a country's suicide rate is indicative of major social change. He believed that the more integrated a person was in society or with smaller groups within society, the lower the likelihood of that person committing suicide. Suicide varies in inverse proportion to the level of integration of social groups (Durkheim, 1952).

Many theories supporting this belief have been put forward regarding the isolating factors associated with greater urbanisation and with a decrease in traditional values such as churchgoing, which promoted stronger social bonds through regular meetings. The ability to feel supported and to access such support is crucial to the ability to manage stressful life situations. Factors that may isolate people, such as being foreign born, unmarried or living alone, are more common in depressives who commit suicide than those who do not (McKeown, 1998).

Poverty, marginalisation, social or economic disadvantage and overcrowded housing are other social conditions that have been linked to suicide.

Unemployment

Unemployment has been shown to be an important risk factor for suicide, with *Suicide in Ireland: A National Study* showing that over a quarter of suicides were unemployed, more likely to be male, and over half of those who were unemployed were out of work for over one year. Employment not only serves an economic function but it is also a source of status, social meaning and purpose. Having been educated to work, the vision of a future without employment may lead to a sense of hopelessness and, therefore, suicide. See Chapter 8 for more on depression related to economic circumstances.

Age

Between 2002 and 2006 the highest rate of suicide for the overall population was among 20-24 year olds, at 20.3 per 100,000. The peak for females was in their early fifties at 8.3

per 100,000, while the peak for males was between 20 and 24 years of age and the rate has risen to 35.3 per 100,000 (National Office for Suicide Prevention, 2008).

In a European comparison, Ireland is twenty-first out of 26 countries as regards the suicide rate for the total population. However, in a European comparison of youth suicide rates (15–24-year-olds), Ireland alarmingly climbs to fourth position out of the same 26 countries (National Office for Suicide Prevention, 2008).

The question as to why so many young people resort to suicide still remains largely unanswered. There are lists of potentially suicidal characteristics and groups that have been identified as being more at risk. However, it must be asked if there is enough being done to help young people and to prevent so many of our young people ending their own lives.

Gender

Gender is a significant factor to consider, with males four times more likely to kill themselves than females in Ireland. In 2004, 406 males killed themselves compared to 87 females for the same year. While in 2008, 332 males killed themselves compared to 92 females for the same period. Some reasons for this were put forward by the Irish National Task Force on Suicide (1998), which suggested that men are more susceptible to risk taking, aggressive and anti-social behaviour, drug abuse and depression. They have greater familiarity with more lethal techniques and they tend to choose more violent methods when attempting suicide.

Many men believe that rational and logical thought is the best way to understand life and that vulnerability, feelings and emotions are to be avoided at all costs. They can think that seeking help and support is a sign of weakness and incompetence, and control of self and others is essential to feel safe (O'Neill, 1995). However, if a problem evokes various feelings for a man which he doesn't acknowledge or want to deal with, this may lead him to hopelessness as he has not learned how to live with these emotions. When a problem cannot be solved by the usual methods, a man may feel uneasy about this perceived lack of control, and trying to control something that you have no power to change, such as another person, is a certain path to self-destruction and continued anxiety (O'Neill et al., 1995). Without the knowledge of how to deal with emotions, men may experience a sense of being out of control, which, through being unable to deal with that, may lead them to believe that control is impossible, thus giving them a sense of hopelessness. Certain problems can seem to become insurmountable, and suicide may seem the only way out of an impossible position.

I conducted research a number of years ago among males aged between 18 and 29 where I found a significant correlation between restrictive emotionality and eventual suicide. Poor problem-solvers have consistently been linked with suicidal behaviour, and, with men denying themselves the hugely significant coping strategy of emotional expression, suicide becomes even more likely.

Hopelessness

Hopelessness is defined as a profound sense of the impossible; a thought process that expects nothing; and a behavioural process in which the person attempts little or takes inappropriate action. Having feelings of hopelessness has been consistently shown to be one of the best predictors of eventual suicide, with the correlation between hopeless-ness and suicide significantly higher than the correlation between depression and suicide (Beck et al., 1985). It has been suggested that those with a small repertoire of coping skills, poor problem-solvers and rigid thinkers may have increased susceptibility to feelings of hopelessness.

Drugs

There is an increased risk of suicide among a drug-using population, with the suicide rate among intravenous drug users estimated to be well in excess of twenty-five times that of the general population. It must also be noted that the mortality rate among drug users is higher than that of the general population, and that many of the factors asso-ciated with suicide are also associated with drug misuse.

These include mental illness, physical health problems, volatile behaviour, bereavement, social isolation, antisocial behaviour, risk-taking behaviours, poor family relation-ships, stressful life events, unemployment, poor social functioning, poor health (and not reporting it or dealing with it), depression, anxiety and hopelessness. Alcoholics and other substance abusers can also be stigmatised and become detached from conventional society. The negative attitudes of other people can exacerbate their sense of alien-ation and therefore discourage them from seeking help for their problems.

Harris and Barraclough (1997) report that the suicide risk for prescription drug abuse alone is twenty times greater than the average rate, when combined with alcohol abuse it was sixteen times greater, and when combined with illicit drug abuse it was forty-four times the expected rate. With multi-drug abuse having one of the highest suicide risks associated with psychiatric disorders, this calls for a need for greater awareness of the high levels of undetected mental illness among drug users. Many theorists believe that addiction is a form of self-medication, so, therefore, treatments need to access, treat or at least name these underlying conditions if an addict is to have any hope of achieving the peace of mind that they desire. This is referred to as dual-diagnosis. It may seem like quite an obvious approach, but dual-diagnosis still evokes argument among those who treat addiction: some support it, while others believe that the sole focus of therapy should be on the addiction itself.

An Irish National Suicide Study (2001) found that almost half of the suicides for 1997 and 1998 were known by their GP or psychiatrist to have attended for alcohol counselling, with those who had gone through marital separation four times more likely to have a history of alcohol abuse. Almost 21 per cent were known to have taken alcohol immediately prior to their suicide, with males, especially those under twenty-five years of age, more likely than females to use alcohol immediately prior to their deaths. The relationship between alcohol and suicide is often quite complex in that the individual may have been suffering the consequences of alcoholism or attempting to self-medicate for depression or another emotional difficulty. Alcohol can give some relief initially, but it frequently produces a depressive effect on the brain, which exacerbates the harmful effects on a brain already experiencing biochemical changes associated with depression (McKeon, 1998).

Poor Problem Solving

As mentioned, limited social problem-solving abilities, interpersonal problem-solving deficits, cognitive rigidity and poor abilities for those under high life stress have all been linked to suicidal behaviour. Schotte and Clum (1982) conducted research which suggests that poor problem solving may play a role in the development of suicidal thoughts, but that it is probably in conjunction with negative life stress that poor problem solving might lead to suicide intent. They find that students with suicidal thoughts were more hopeless, and that both cognitively rigid individuals under high stress and poor problem solvers were significantly more hopeless. They also suggest that some individuals may be cognitively unprepared to develop effective alternative solutions necessary to cope with stressors in their environment.

Access to Methods of Suicide

Much of the literature suggests that limiting access to various means of committing suicide can reduce suicide rates. However, this may be difficult, if not impossible. The idea is supported by a striking reduction in suicides during the mid-1960s in Britain, which is attributed largely to the detoxification of the domestic gas supply. Similar changes occurred in Australia with restrictions on the prescribing of barbiturates, in the USA with the introduction of catalytic converters and in Canada with the introduction of gun control laws.

Other Factors

Alienation, worthlessness, despair and guilt are all powerful emotions that have been associated with suicide, as have a negative self-image, low self-esteem and negative expectancies about life. Early school leavers, victims of sexual, physical or emotional abuse, people who immerse themselves too much in the past, and those suffering from marital breakdown are also believed to be more at risk than the general population. Negative life stress – events that shatter core beliefs or the defining worth of an individual – can trigger suicidal tendencies. For women, interpersonal stressors can be influential, while, for men, stressors associated with achievement can lead to suicidal thoughts.

What to Do if You Are Suicidal

If you are suicidal, it is important to immediately avail of whatever support is accessible to you before you quickly fall into hopelessness. Talking about and naming our problems can have a surprisingly beneficial effect on our seemingly permanent agony. Try to remember that most of life's difficulties do have solutions and that all of our feelings will change, including the bad ones. This is very difficult to remember and believe when we are in the pits of despair. However, there is only one certainty in life and only one thing that I can actually promise to you right now: everything changes.

As I noted earlier, we know that good moods will change but we believe that bad ones will last forever. This is a lie. There is only one constant in life and that is change. This means that even the darkest of all our emotions will lift at some stage and we will most likely feel content again at some point in our lives. This is true.

What to Do if You Know Someone Who Is Suicidal

A cry for help always needs a response and all hints of suicide need to be taken seriously. Below is a list of what you can do if someone you know is suicidal. Reading through the following may also help someone who is suicidal.

- Always take the person seriously; believe what it is they are saying
- Listen; don't jump in quickly with advice or opinions
- Don't interrogate or analyse
- Ask caring questions: don't be afraid to ask what is wrong, whether the person is suicidal or even whether they have a particular plan or method in mind
- Judgements or categorisation can cause great irritation
- Most suicidal people do not want to be alone
- Form an empathic and supportive relationship
- Don't argue someone out of suicide
- Try not to be shocked by what the person says
- Don't belittle or dismiss their feelings
- Don't advise, compare or criticise
- Avoid false reassurances; be as honest as possible
- Any focus on hope must be based on reality
- Let them know that feelings are temporary, that depression can be treated and that problems can be solved
- Show them that they are not alone and that you are there for them
- Don't patronise or pity the person
- Ask them for alternatives to this course of action
- Show that you are available rather than trying to take charge

- Show that you care and can be trusted
- Do not normalise or sensationalise suicide
- Sharing your appropriate knowledge of suicide may help to break down some of the myths and prevent a suicide
- Form a suicide contract. This is a promise by the suicidal individual to contact you before they try to kill themselves. Make a list of other contacts just in case you or another contact is unavailable
- Make a list of potential sources of support from friends to professionals to support groups such as The Samaritans
- Don't rush the person; give them space to express themselves in their own time
- Suicide should not be seen as an easy way out of difficulties; it should be seen as a manifestation of psychological problems
- Show that you identify with the person's emotional state, if possible and appropriate
- Encourage the person to seek professional help and accompany them if that's what they need to make the first contact. They may need support in continuing to seek professional help
- Evaluate the immediacy of the danger of the threat

If the person is in immediate danger:

- Do not leave them alone until help is available
- Remove all potential aids to suicide such as drugs, firearms, razors or knives
- Medication may be necessary until the crisis abates
- Contact the local doctor

- If the doctor is unavailable, go to the nearest hospital, clinic or psychiatric facility
- If the above are unavailable, ring the local emergency number or contact the local Gardaí who may be able to assist

Bereavement Due to Suicide

Bereavement due to death from natural causes can involve various stages of grief. However, bereavement due to death by suicide can intensify all these emotional experiences and this can make the process even more difficult to undergo. Many people don't experience bereavement stages in the order stated below: some will move back and forth between stages, while others will skip some stages altogether or even experience ones that are not mentioned. It is important to remember that all movement and change in the grieving process is of benefit to that individual.

1. *Shock and denial*: this can be experienced in any form, from a complete denial of what has happened to a reluctance to feel the emotion on a deep level
2. *Angry sadness*: anger and resentment are natural phases of grief; this anger can become quite explosive and can be directed at anyone
3. *Guilt and bargaining*: this is sometimes referred to as the 'what ifs'. Many people can torment themselves during this phase in an attempt to erase their upset with what they didn't do when the person was alive
4. *Depression*: despair, remorse, emptiness, loneliness and hopelessness are all significant emotions that many bereaved people go through

5. *Elation*: this can be very confusing for many people, as happy emotions in the middle of grief just don't seem to fit. However, this is an emotion that many people report feeling in waves

6. *Withdrawal*: avoidance of social occasions, isolation and withdrawal from various relationships can be common among the bereaved

7. *Acceptance*: this phase can begin slowly and may also be accompanied by anxiety and guilt about beginning to feel happy again. Hope and contentment can begin to soften the sense of loss and, although cycles of grief can still hit the person, acceptance does bring a reprieve from the pain

Your experience of grief can be a very personal one and it is important not to avoid the intense pain that can be involved in the grieving process. Many people report periods of confusion and disorganisation, with distress hitting them in waves followed by some relief. Physical symptoms are also common: sleeplessness, shortness of breath, diarrhoea, back and neck pain – to name but a few. People can experience a range of emotions, from happiness (perhaps due to memories of the deceased) to despair and intense sadness. You may feel peculiar at times, but it is important to remember that everything that you experience is a normal reaction.

Suffering the death of a loved one by suicide not only intensifies the above reactions but also brings with it many additional burdens. The 'survivors' are the relatives, friends and acquaintances of a suicide victim, and their grieving process can be much more difficult because of the following:

- Stigma from civil and religious authorities, from the general public and, more recently, from psychological suicide theories suggesting parent–child relationship difficulties as a cause of suicide

- Support was historically denied to survivors by the laws of the land and by organised religion. Nowadays, there may be much uncertainty, fear and discomfort in friends and relatives who would normally have given more support

- It is estimated that less than 15 per cent of suicide victims leave a note. Survivors can be left with a great mystery surrounding the death of a loved one, and this can make the mourning process last longer

- Survivors can experience great anger at what they may feel is the ultimate selfish act. Guilt about speaking ill of the dead may keep these difficult emotions repressed and cause other psychological problems for the survivor

- If the victim was a burden to the family, there may also be guilt at feeling a sense of relief

- Saying goodbye to a person who you know is going to die can help significantly in the grieving process. In the case of suicide, this can be complicated by the victim saying goodbye to close friends and relatives without them knowing

- The person who finds the body is often left with a lifetime of haunting images

- Survivors' health problems may get considerably worse after the suicide of someone close to them

- Because suicide is seldom talked about, there can be less assistance in the form of literature or support groups

- The victim's family suffers a tremendous shock and they frequently move house to avoid the social stigma
- The survivors may brood excessively about the death, often losing faith and trust in themselves and others

The majority of professionals believe that it essential for survivors to talk about the death, that the word 'suicide' should be used and that feelings and thoughts need to be shared. Life needs to be kept as normal as possible after the acute grief. You should express your needs clearly and honestly, and allow yourself to be part of a group of people who care. Children experience similar feelings and they should be included in conversations, they should be listened to and the expression of their emotions encouraged through games and drawings. Accidents are more common during stressful periods, so extra care is needed; and time needs to be taken out to think, rest and sleep.

The mourning process is greatly extended when death is due to suicide, yet the social stigma associated with suicide encourages survivors to end the mourning period more quickly than would be usual. Survivors need to treat their grief with the attention it deserves.

Suicide has been viewed as an escape from emotional pain, as retaliation, as an effort to make amends for wrongs, and as a desire to rejoin a deceased person. It has been seen by some as a praiseworthy act, as an effort to force love from others, as an attempt to induce guilt in others, as an act of war, such as suicide bombing, and as an escape from aversive self-awareness.

Although some people will threaten suicide but never make an attempt and some will self-harm with tablets or by cutting themselves, all attempts and threats need to be taken seriously as it is impossible to predict who will complete the act.

Depression leading to a desperate hopelessness is the best indicator of whether someone will commit suicide. The key is to notice and interrupt this process early enough. If someone is suicidal, many of the techniques discussed in this book would be of great benefit to them.

Summary

- Suicide is now accepted in Ireland as the principal cause of death in young people, and the rate of suicide has exceeded death due to road traffic accidents since 1997

- Throughout history, suicide has been both commended and condemned and, in Ireland, suicide remained a crime until 1993

- There are a number of theories attempting to explain suicidal behaviour. However, there are many myths about suicide that only create confusion and ignorance

- Warning signs and factors associated with suicide may help to foresee a potential suicide, but the prediction of a suicide is practically impossible for all family, friends, relatives and also professionals in the field

- All hints of suicide need to be taken seriously and there are various dos and don'ts when dealing with a suicidal person

- Bereavement due to death by suicide will exaggerate the grieving experiences and stages that a person may go through, compared to a death from natural causes. Added to this are many other burdening factors that can extend the mourning process and make it more difficult to get through the grief

8

Depression Due to Unemployment and Financial Circumstances

Introduction

At the time of writing this book, the world was experiencing a global economic meltdown, and Ireland was experiencing a more severe recession than most other western countries. In my own practice I have seen an increase in depression and anxiety among my clients with direct links to economic worries and fears. They talk about future fears, unfairness in society, perceived corruption of some politicians and some bankers, and the proliferation of bad news through the media. The depressing effects have been reaching everyone, even those not directly affected by the economic downturn. Too much consistent bad news has been depressing the entire nation.

Although the issues discussed in this chapter relate primarily to a society and individual affected by recession, most of these concerns can also affect any individual experiencing financial difficulties at any other period. The triggers and consequences expressed are relevant in a recession, but a family or an individual can experience recession at any time in their lives. Anyone can fall into financial difficulty, even while those around them may be thriving. The issues described below are triggered by economic circumstances, both national and individual, and they affect us to the core of our vulnerability in that they disrupt and upset our ability to survive.

In a society in economic recession, people are losing their jobs and with that their financial security and their hopes and dreams for the future. Of course, losing your job at any time is a distressing event. It can bring new and serious fears into your life: the fear of losing your house; the dread of having to significantly change your lifestyle; the anxiety of having no health insurance; and the worry of having to pay the utility bills and somehow find money to buy food for the week. These situations can lead to a person becoming depressed.

Pecuniary difficulties can also lead to a reduced social life and the subsequent loss of the relaxing effects of socialising. People can feel embarrassed at having to leave a club due to not being able to pay fees, not being able to join friends for lunch or having to work at a job that they previously would have looked down on. Friends can get pushed into the background due to new time constraints or lack of money for socialising. This creates a situation where depression can take hold.

In addition to financial losses, people's identities can also suffer. The job that gave them so much pride in themselves is now defunct, and perhaps it is now necessary for the ageing person to have to reinvent themselves all over again. Many people value themselves on the basis of their job or their breadwinner role and so loss of this can lead to a substantial reduction in self-esteem and depression.

In times of economic uncertainty, all of us experience emotional turmoil related to job losses, anxious work environments and the fear of increased burglaries. We pick up on the distress of those close to us, whether it's expressed or hidden.

Our days are full of bad news, from job losses to the seemingly unjust protection of politicians and bankers who have their fingerprints all over the root causes of our specific problems. The psychological impact on the individual of economic decline in a country as a whole cannot be underestimated. In economic terms, this impact on the individual can manifest itself in plunging consumer confidence, a situation that can perpetuate the economic crisis.

Below, I'll look at some of the causes of depression due to reduced financial circumstances and recession and then at the effects these can have on us as individuals. By identifying the causes and the effects, this may help us to somewhat alleviate our resultant depression by learning how to manage and deal with it. There seems to be little or no research done on this type of depression. I see variations in the mindset of people presenting to me in work with depression due to economic circumstances: previously positive people view the world very negatively and people with usually healthy coping skills find themselves stuck in an ever-repeating cycle of negative irrational thinking that just feeds their anxiety and depression. This kind of depression needs further consideration as a more creative approach may be needed to find solutions and to help treat it.

Unemployment and Financial Circumstances as Triggers for Depression

There are a certain amount of causes or triggers that can be common to all of us, but each individual has unique levels of tolerance and vulnerability, and the same triggers can affect people in different ways. Depression and anxiety are common consequences, but some may experience such extremes of stress and panic that they require hospitalisation. Many of these emotions also seem to create a chain reaction where they spill over into relationships and friendships and create discord, paranoia and depression in emotionally connected individuals. The following triggers can apply to any individual in difficult financial circumstances or who has just lost their job.

Job Loss and Financial Concerns

These have been discussed above. With job loss and the subsequent adjustment to lifestyles, the whole family can suffer embarrassment in front of their friends and relatives. Kids who were used to all the latest styles now become the unfashionable ones who they might have poked fun at before. Parents suffer the embarrassment of being on view in the very long and public dole queues. These stories are depressing to hear but devastating to have to live.

For those who have serious financial concerns, they just don't go away. Many households may be unable to pay their mortgages and, with a large percentage perhaps in negative equity, there may be no way out of the red.

Faced with unpaid bills, hungry mouths and an increasing debt with no way out, people can become desperate. They can experience hopelessness and suicide could become a new thought for some.

Reinventing Yourself

During boom times there is usually an increased need for some professions, with attractive remunerations and great prospects for the future. Many of these professions either disappear or are scaled back significantly in a recession. The upshot of this is that many people find that their newly acquired skills have become obsolete.

It's back to square one if you are lucky, but if you are anywhere near the end of your working career the prospect of finding another job or career is probably null and void. Losing a job also means losing a community of people, social status, a daily routine and a sense of control. The idea of reinventing yourself is a daunting prospect, but having to let go of a career and job that you trained so hard to obtain can be something akin to a death and, for some, a grieving process may ensue.

Too Much Time

With job losses and reduced working hours, many people have additional free time on their hands. This can be something people long for but, when it becomes a reality, it does bring with it many unforeseen difficulties.

It is commonly known that a high percentage of men die in the first two years of their retirement; this seems to highlight the shock and emotional strain when a person, who has worked so consistently for so long, suddenly stops working. It may also suggest that people need to prepare for a different lifestyle, and they need to learn how to wind down to a slower pace of life. However, for someone who has lost their job this can be impossible. They now have the added difficulty of too much time and no distractions from their ever-increasing stress and worry. Many turn to desperate measures in order to cope.

Avoidance Coping

The sudden burden of all of the above can be an immense weight for any of us to carry. Some can take to bed, while others use alcohol and other drugs in a vain attempt to ignore their stresses and move on with life. It is generally accepted that avoidance and disengagement are adverse coping skills with damaging consequences for the individual. By trying to avoid the unavoidable, we are guaranteeing some form of psychological upset that will just compound our problems. However, it is important to note that avoidance of persistent negative thinking through distraction is an extremely beneficial coping method with many advantageous consequences. It is important for us to determine when our methods of avoidance are of benefit to us or to our detriment. This can be done by looking at the consequences of our behaviour in different situations.

Paranoia

This is a state of mind that many people become accustomed to during a recession. The threat of unemployment can hang over everyone's head and there is a general fear of underperforming at work or not having enough to do. Employees constantly try to interpret their managers' expressions and read between the lines of everything that they say. This anxiety instils fear, depression and paranoia.

In this context, Sunday night can bring gloom, anxiety and worry about the week ahead. The stress of preparing ourselves for a working week, after the comforts and safety of the weekend, can be a significant depressive trigger for many of us.

Consequences

Suicide, murder and cardiovascular disease are all believed to increase during a recession. The number of burglaries, kidnappings, incidents of domestic violence and bank robberies all increase in a recession; however, though the factors that influence crime rates are varied and complex, it is generally believed that financial difficulty is a major trigger.

There can also be other factors in any society at any given time that can contribute to such trends. An increase in alcohol consumption may be an attempt to cope with the adverse effects of a recession and may lead directly to violent behaviour. However, an increase in heroin consumption could, for instance, be solely linked to a significant increase in supply.

Whether related to the recession or not, in my own practice I have recently seen an increase in depression and anxiety and a significant increase in gambling addiction. Perhaps gambling is an attempt to make money. It does seem to be an attempt to avoid difficulties, created by the recession or otherwise. Gambling is a particularly destructive addiction. Absolutely everything a person owns can be lost, and relatives can see no signs of the impending devastation. This is an industry with strong lobbying powers, late opening hours, increased ease of access and no health warnings. There are inadequate restrictions and paltry regulations.

I see the effects of economic uncertainty, both individual and national, on two different but interconnected levels: these are the obvious emotional consequences and the cognitive effects relating to our beliefs and judgements.

Emotional and Physical Consequences

The main emotional consequences of financial difficulty are obvious to all of us: anxiety, worry and concern for our livelihoods, fear that we won't be able to survive and feed our dependants, and stress and apprehension at what the future might bring. We can all feel the effects. Those who are financially secure can worry about those friends and family who are less fortunate.

While such emotions make sense in these situations, it is the breadth and depth of them that seem unique to financial pressures and changes in financial situations. In my work, as I mentioned, I see previously positive people become hopeless, and previously optimistic people become deeply depressed. Some fall so hard that cognitive therapy is lost on them, as rational logic becomes an unintelligible language. The incidence of this type of upset seems to increase in a recession and I have seen people get stuck in a dark circle of self-defeating statements and depression. It is an emotional space that they have no experience of, and this apparent loss of control feeds severe anxiety, panic and further depression. Some can relate their distress directly to their economic concerns, while others focus on unresolved past issues or present seemingly unrelated anxieties, or direct energy towards potential catastrophic outcomes. This misdirection of an individual's energy and focus can make their recovery a bit more complicated and it can therefore take longer.

The emotional consequences of a financial plunge not only hit hard but they also strike many areas of a person's life, such as their relationships. Many who had planned to separate can become unable to afford the inevitable, and the stress and strain of this affects the entire family.

There is also an increase in people who are suffering what is called compassion fatigue. This is found where a carer or those in the caring profession give so much with little coming back in form of recognition, empathy and resources; such people may also be affected by having exposure to the trauma of others. Compassion fatigue may involve a general lethargy that can leave a person feeling exhausted and unable to complete their everyday tasks. Their reluctance to engage with family and friends may leave them even more isolated and depressed.

It is widely accepted that the body will manifest what the mind has difficulty in coming to terms with. Tension can cause back and neck pain, and stress can be the cause of stomach ulcers, migraines, and general pains and aches. Experiencing difficult emotions due to financial worries can lead to physical consequences. However, exercise can alleviate physical discomfort and become a coping skill in itself. Indeed, people may find that they now have enough time to perfect their sport or train for a marathon.

Cognitive Consequences

A considerable change in our economic circumstances can challenge many of our previously held beliefs and judgements. We might question our existence and our raison d'être and re-evaluate what is important to us. Through my clients and patients, I am seeing a portion of this thinking, and it is predominantly of a positive nature. I have seen people readjust their priorities and move away from aesthetics and acquisition of wealth to spending time with family and friends, and the pleasure that good company brings.

People can hold very strong ideas about what they believe to be important and also what might give them value as a person. Many consider wealth to be desirable and something that can bestow great value on the individual: 'If I am rich, then people will like me, and if people like me then I will feel good about myself.'

Many believe that their career and their success in that career will also give them value and help them to feel good about themselves. The loss of these self-defining beliefs can leave people reeling in an abyss of fear without the usual reinforcements of their perceived worth.

This irrational and distorted thinking was discussed in Chapters 3 and 5, and it can be a major cause of depression. The loss of wealth and social stature can lead people to challenge the importance of these things in their lives. This can cause considerable stress and result in deep depression, especially if there is no alternative thinking to take the place of these ideologies.

People's prejudices can also be challenged if, for instance, they take what they might consider to be a lesser job. The resultant attitude of their friends may prove to be a massive eye-opener, with some friends rejecting them outright and others letting the friendship fall by the wayside. True mediocrity and weakness of character may be displayed in those who they may have thought to be real friends.

What We Can Do

The re-evaluation of what matters in life is, on the surface, a noble pursuit. It can be quite a difficult process to change judgements and let go of beliefs that may have formed the foundation of your character. However, often such adjustments to our thinking are beneficial and make us happier.

You might come to the conclusion that value and worth may not lie in certain careers, but in, for example, growing your own vegetables. Perhaps, as a society, we might find that displays of wealth are vulgar when once they were to be envied. We might think that lower paid and more stable jobs are more attractive than insecure and volatile high-earning jobs. Perhaps we are seeing the return of sincere and genuine attributes of respect, compassion and thoughtfulness as admirable qualities compared to the ostentation and pretence that predominated during the boom.

Many of the techniques already discussed in this book can help with depression due to financial crisis: making an effort to fill our time, being careful not to feed our depression with negative thinking, doing exercise and many other ideas can be useful to all of us at any given time. It is important to note that most of us can be affected in some way by an economic slump, be it directly or indirectly through the experience of others, or even through listening to too many news reports.

There are, however, some specific coping skills worth considering:

- With a job loss, the ensuing spare time can be dangerous. We should occupy our time appropriately by playing with the kids, exercising and doing all those things that we wished we could do instead of going to work. Investigating new potentials for earning a wage is a positive use of our spare time and a necessary exercise for many of us. Although we may mourn the loss of a career and the community and status that it brought, it is important to move towards letting go of the past and to focus on what needs to be done in the future. Everything changes and, if we don't learn to adapt, things will get worse for us and the people who are closest to us

- We can get stuck in negative thinking and negative conversations. We can dwell on anything from the colossal mess that the banks created to the person who parks in the space for disabled drivers. People can engage in obnoxious behaviour, but we need to look at our own hypocrisy first and change our own behaviour before we can justify throwing stones at other people. Positive thinking is vital in a recession. We might have concerns and worries, but our negative thoughts can create many more, leading to deeper depression. This was discussed in detail in Chapter 5. A previous client of mine noted to me how he was struggling through the recession like everyone else, but he was enjoying the little things more. I believe his focus on the positive smaller things in life to be a significant coping skill that we can all use for ourselves

- Quite simply, being nice to each other can reduce our sense of annoyance and anxiety, and promote a better overall feeling. As soon as we realise that we are all in this together, we may then begin to develop a sense of community where we can help each other. Letting someone out in traffic does have a positive consequence for all concerned, and the act of saying hello and stopping to enquire after a neighbour has a very positive effect on our mood. These actions are impossible to quantify, but we all know that they feel good and they have the possibility of being contagious. A strong sense of community is widely accepted to be a very effective coping skill in dealing with adversity

- We need to laugh. The Irish have coped with much hardship and one of our best coping skills is to make fun of even the most gruelling of situations. Laughter is believed to be one of the most effective of coping skills. Making people laugh is something that the Irish are good at. We need to make this effort. It will lift our spirits

Summary

- Unemployment and changed financial circumstances, and the life adjustments relating to these, are common triggers for depression in individuals. Therefore, if a country is going through a recession, the number of cases of such depression increases

- Such depression can be experienced in different strengths, either directly by individuals or vicariously through the experiences of those close to us

- This type of depression can be very difficult to deal with seeing as it directly affects our and our family's ability to survive. As well as emotional, physical and cognitive consequences, there also seem to be other distinctive effects for the individual, such as a rise in cardiovascular disease

- There are some distinctive skills for trying to manage depression due to economic circumstances

9

Continued Recovery

As regards depression, wanting and being able to seek help is essential in the ongoing management of our moods. People can sometimes resist seeking help, which ultimately only serves to prolong the agony of a desperate situation. Without the support and guidance of family, friends and professionals, people can become even more isolated in their torment, believing their problems to be unsolvable. This can lead to hopelessness and potential suicide.

Help can come in many forms – from a self-help book such as this to family or friends. The fact that you are reading this book means that you have actively sought to manage your depression, which is a great start. I suggest, however, that appropriate professional help is probably the best course of action. By appropriate I mean that one-to-one and group psychotherapy and counselling is always a prudent choice. However, there may be occasions when a doctor or psychiatrist may be needed in order to dispense drugs. This may be necessary in situations where the individual has become so entrenched in their darkness that logical reasoning or rational thought is unachievable until the person is able to rise out of it.

We will look at some of the factors involved in seeking help. Therefore, if, for instance, someone you know is resisting help, this might identify the nature of their resistance and challenge their attitudes and behaviour so that they can better help themselves. If they are aware of their barriers to seeking help, they may be able to change them or go around them, and then point themselves towards the light and a better existence. I cannot emphasis enough that seeking help is most definitely the best step you can take in learning how to manage your depression and living a more happy and content life.

Help-Seeking Behaviour

Attitudes, beliefs and predicted outcomes all play a role in the decision process of whether or not to seek help. People with a positive attitude and confidence in professional help are going to be more willing to seek help for psychological problems. Those unconcerned with the perceived stigma attached to seeking professional psychological help will be more likely to seek it. A person's beliefs in how emotional problems develop can determine whether they will look for help in the form of drugs, psychotherapy or a close friend.

Preferred Sources of Help

Data from a variety of sources indicates that the vast majority of people with distress do not seek professional treatment (over 70 per cent). Studies indicate a primary reliance on informal support rather than formal support, with the majority of people preferring to turn to a spouse or friends in times of worry or unhappiness. For coping with persistent problems, people indicate that they would seek some form of professional help, with doctors, clergy, psychologists, psychiatrists and psychotherapists being among the most popular. It is also widely thought that where the person turns for help depends on the severity of the problem, with a relative shift from clergy to doctors to psychologists as the problem becomes more severe or more specific.

Data also shows that the probability of someone seeking help markedly increases when the potential helper is a friend. The preference for seeking help from informal sources may be partly explained by the easy accessibility of family and friends, by the emotional support given, and by the lack of cost involved. Another aspect of informal networks is that they involve enduring relationships with a history of intimacy, self-disclosure and reciprocal help. A person would be encouraged to seek support within an equal relationship where there is mutual seeking and giving of help.

Social Context and Age

Studies have shown that high support through marital satisfaction and availability of confidants outside the family can mean that people do not seek help from professionals. This suggests that social support operates to reduce psychological distress, providing a source of active help and a buffer against life stress.

Data concerned with age has typically shown a decline in formal help-seeking as a person gets older.

Socioeconomic Status

Research suggests a socioeconomic differential with regard to help-seeking. This difference may be due to increased access to health services, more positive attitudes to psychotherapy in higher socioeconomic classes, and may also be due to the fact that income and education are related to greater levels of well-being and also to higher rates of help-seeking. It has also been shown that clients have achieved the greatest depth of self-exploration when working with a therapist of the same social class and racial background. This may suggest a level of understanding between the client and professional, greater empathy on the part of the professional because of this understanding, and the influence of the perceived level of equality between the therapist and client.

Visibility of Help-Seeking

The act of seeking help can be viewed as an admission of inferiority, inadequacy or dependency, and may also be a source of stigma and embarrassment, especially among men. It is therefore generally believed that help-seeking increases as the number of people who know about the request for help decreases. This factor may also help to explain the high prevalence of help-seeking within informal social networks such as friends and spouses.

Controllability of the Problem

Perceptions of the problem as uncontrollable seem to increase help-seeking, perhaps because this reduces the resulting panic and stress, and also reduces the threat to self-esteem such as the feeling of inadequacy that deters help-seeking. People who see the solution to their problems as under their control may be more willing to seek the sort of help in which they are integral in finding, providing and implementing their own solutions.

Previous Experience and the Ability of the Helper

More often than not, people seek help because they are unable to manage or solve their problems. Whether people are motivated to ask for help may depend on their previous experience of such help and whether it was effective. For instance, if previous experiences of therapy were primarily positive, then people may look again for this type of help.

A therapist's perceived expertise, trustworthiness, regard, empathy, genuineness and general helpfulness can influence a client's willingness to return for a second session and what a client expects in terms of improvement. Therapists who are skilled at communicating empathy, a desire to help and an understanding of the client's problem, and who avoid hostility and moralising, are especially successful at influencing clients to enter and continue treatment, and, indeed, in gaining successful outcomes.

Gender Issues

As discussed earlier, men are often encouraged not to express emotions or any weakness and, implicit in this, not to seek help. Men are traditionally taught to be silent about any emotional difficulty. They are encouraged to show a strong and controlled image to the world, which is seen as inconsistent with asking for help, a sign of weakness. It has been reported that two-thirds of all clients seeking psychological help are female, with one in three women compared with one in seven men seeking services from a mental health professional at some point during their lifetime.

Other Factors

People who are interested in hearing honest feedback about themselves are particularly likely to seek psychological help, whereas people who rate achievement highly are significantly less likely to seek help. Perhaps they see help-seeking as a threat to high achievement and an indicator of failure. Although individuals with high self-esteem are more reluctant to seek help, they may be motivated to do so when the embarrassment of being consistently unable to solve the problem supersedes the perceived threat to their self-esteem. Shy people may also sometimes avoid social interaction, and because help-seeking often involves initiating a social interaction, this can be a problem.

Signs of Relapse

When we begin to feel good again after a period of depression, a lot of us can let go of the reins and this can lead us to return to our old ways of thinking and behaving. Although we all can become depressed at different times in our lives, it is very important to keep up our more balanced lifestyle and our positive ways of thinking and being, otherwise we risk becoming more depressed more often.

It is initially very important to increase our awareness of symptoms and signs of an impending depression. With this knowledge we can then change our behaviour and use our supports in the hope that we may interrupt the cycle before the depression really sets in. Some indicators of depression returning include:

- Depressive mood
- Loss of interest and/or withdrawal from usual activities
- Harmful and detrimental sleeping and/or eating patterns
- Compulsive/impulsive behaviour
- Confusion, inability to concentrate or focus attention
- Apathy or laziness
- Being easily irritated and angered
- Poor judgement and decision making
- Lack or loss of self-confidence
- Substance use to elevate mood
- Hopelessness, meaninglessness and helplessness
- Avoidance of treatment plan and daily routine
- Loss of libido
- Denial of impending depression
- Tense muscles: neck, shoulders, etc.
- Loss of energy
- Loss of appetite
- Signs of stress such as dry mouth, unsettled stomach, constriction in chest, or shortness of breath and changes in breathing

A strategy may be to recognise our usual reaction to any of the above and then identify a more effective response with more beneficial consequences. We also need to be aware of what supports we can use and how those close to us could help. It is very important to keep noting what works and what doesn't work: remember that everything changes and you may need to change routines and activities to suit your needs at different times.

Techniques for Further Managing Depression

Time Management

Designing and implementing an individualised time management system that fits your own personality can be a great support in continuing to deal with and manage your depression. This includes work, everyday chores, exercise, leisure and free time, which all need to be scheduled in to achieve a balanced lifestyle. However, before doing this we need to become aware of our many self-defeating statements relating to time:

'If I only had more time.'

'There aren't enough hours in the day.'

'My time isn't my own.'

These negative thoughts border on being irrational, and they can eventually lead us to feel hopeless. Once they are put in perspective with statements based on our real circumstances, this will help us to manage our time more effectively. Suggestions to help with this are listed below:

- Be realistic with how much you can actually achieve in a given time period
- Prioritise the most important tasks
- Be aware of times when your energy is high and low and do the more difficult tasks during your peak performance phase

- Identify the best use of your time at a particular stage
- Delegate responsibilities to others
- Remember that perfection may not be necessary, so be happy when you achieve the results that you were looking for
- Make decisions quickly to save energy and time for more important tasks
- Make use of waiting time and do smaller tasks
- Break larger jobs into smaller and more achievable ones
- Set goals and reward yourself when these are accomplished
- Remind yourself of the benefits of completing the task
- Find a place conducive to the completion of the task
- Develop your ability to say 'no' to things that are infringing negatively on your life
- Approach with a positive attitude

Suggestions for Sleep

Getting quality sleep and rest is essential for our physical, mental and emotional health, and sleep or lack of it can be a significant issue for many people who suffer from depression. Below are some suggestions for sleeping soundly:

- Exercise daily and keep a routine that includes work, rest and play
- Try dealing with unresolved issues during the day so your mind doesn't race once your head hits the pillow
- Wake up at the same time every day

- Reduce lighting, noise and visual distractions in your room and try to use it only for sleeping, as the brain may get the message that the room is for other activities or stressful emotions

- Follow a pre-bed routine: reading, stretching, washing, etc.

- Avoid caffeine, tobacco and alcohol late in the day as these will disturb sleep

- Eat a light snack if you feel hungry. Milk and tuna contain L-tryptophan, which helps to induce sleep

- Don't take naps during the day

- Consistently using sleeping tablets can interfere with sleep and leave you groggy the next day

- Engage in a relaxing activity before bedtime

Meditation and Guided Imagery

These exercises are reported by many to be particularly powerful and effective in coping with depression. There are numerous different types of meditations and guided imagery (a programme of directed thoughts and suggestions that guide your imagination towards a relaxed and focused state), all of which you can adapt to suit your needs at any particular time. Below are a number of examples, but be creative in finding an exercise that helps you most.

Ground Yourself

Sit in an upright position with your back straight, your feet on the ground and your hands resting on your thighs. Close your eyes, breathe in through your nose and out through your mouth. Breathe deeply from the bottom of your stomach and find a relaxing rhythm. Note all the noises around you, draw attention to anywhere in your body where you feel tense or stressed and direct your breath towards those areas in order to relax them. Finally and slowly, working from the top of your head down to your toes and back up again, become aware of every part of your body, from the clothes against your skin to the pressure of the chair against your limbs.

Create a Special Place

Find a comfortable position and relax. Imagine yourself in a beautiful place: it could be somewhere that you know, perhaps a mountain you haven't climbed or even the bottom of the sea. Now explore your environment, noticing all the visual details, the sounds and the smells.

You may also want to make it more comfortable by putting a chair or a shelter there, or even surrounding the area with a golden light of protection and safety. This is now your place where you can go to find peace and healing.

Meet Your Inner Guide

Go to your special place (see above) and imagine yourself walking on a path heading towards a bright light. As you get closer you begin to see a person whose details become gradually clearer. Greet this person, ask their name and take whatever name comes to you first; don't worry about it. Walk with them. They may point out parts of your special place that you haven't seen before, or you may just enjoy each other's company. Ask your guide a specific question or whether they have any advice for you; the answer may be immediate or come in some form later. When the experience feels complete, thank your guide and ask them to meet you there again. Open your eyes and return to the outside world.

Self-Appreciation

Picture yourself in an everyday situation and imagine someone you know or perhaps a stranger looking at you with great love and admiration. They tell you something that they really like about you and now a few more people arrive and agree that you are a great person. This may be embarrassing for some people but do try to stick with it. Imagine more and more people arriving with the same love and admiration in their eyes for you. Perhaps you are now on a stage and they are all applauding you, take a bow and thank them.

There are an infinite number of beautiful environments which you could explore in your mind. You could imagine breathing in and out a plethora of colours. You could let go of your problems through imaginary bubbles that disperse and disappear in the wind. You could imagine that you have already realised desired goals, or you could exhale while making a humming noise. Meditations, deep breathing and relaxation can also be added to movement or massage to create self-healing and health-generating techniques.

There are also hundreds of opportunities throughout our daily lives where we can engage in shorter forms of relaxation.

• When sitting at a red light, take a deep breath

- When standing in a queue, rise slowly up onto your toes, breathe deeply and relax
- When watching TV, during each commercial break massage different parts of your body while breathing deeply and relaxing
- At work, take three deep breaths every twenty minutes and gently adjust your posture. Replace stressful thoughts with encouraging inner dialogue
- When on the phone, massage the other ear and shoulder, and take a few deep breaths
- When doing physical work, try to coordinate your movements with your breathing
- When washing your hair, massage your scalp vigorously, rub your ears, relax and take deep breaths

A small amount of daily practice with these exercises can have immense and immediate benefits. Even ten seconds here and there will create a positive change and will awaken the healer within.

Relationships and Living with a Depressive

Relationships can be damaged as a result of depression. Living with a depressive can put a great strain on familial relationships, but an even greater strain on intimate relationships, especially if the other person doesn't understand the dynamics of depression. A depressive can be mentally absent from the relationship for prolonged periods; this can happen without any warning and the effects can be quite traumatic for the other person.

A depressive can be good-humoured, warm, open and caring, and involved in all aspects of life, interacting positively with all those around them, but within a matter of minutes this can change to the complete opposite, with the person becoming withdrawn, reticent, distant or angry. They may physically isolate themselves or remain motionless, making little or no attempt to communicate, interact or respond to any efforts to engage them.

Although a family can get used to this sudden change, it still has detrimental effects on relationships with children, parents, partners and friends. The unpredictability of this transformation, the harshness of the alteration, the suddenness and extreme variation from happiness to misery – this is very challenging to deal with.

People can find it hard to trust a relationship with a depressive. They can adapt to protect themselves against potential hurt and can detach themselves in an attempt to live a more consistently harmonious life.

Living with or being close to a depressive can be demanding. Here are a few tips for coping with it:

- The important first step is to gain an understanding of how the depressive feels and, perhaps more importantly, to let the depressive know how their behaviour affects you. Without this, all individuals are left trying to figure out what is happening. Avoid misconceptions and erroneous beliefs about the depressed person. Accusations, spoken or unspoken, of selfishness, callousness and weirdness only exacerbate an already difficult situation. When people understand what is happening, it can make a situation so much easier to cope with. Openness encourages compassion and possible quicker relief from the situation

- Discuss with the depressive a plan of action for when they are depressed. Some people may need to be on their own, others may need to be occupied while, for many, it can help to just name how they are feeling. It's important that the depressed person has permission to do what is necessary. However, in certain cases, such as family commitments, compromise does need to be achieved

- The depressed person needs to encourage themselves to name their emotions. It is not the partner's role to encourage such expression, but they can help by trying to be understanding of the person's pain, and not make suggestions about how to 'fix' things. The sadness is the depressive's responsibility; they need to work on not wallowing in the darkness and the concerned person needs to work on not absorbing the depression so that it impinges on them. Be aware of emotional boundaries and maintain your own perspective. Sometimes the depressed person may be in a space where they can see little or no positivity at all. This can be quite infectious, and it is essential that a partner holds on to their own view of the world and doesn't let it become skewed by negativity

- Try not to take the depressive's behaviour personally. When a depressed person becomes withdrawn, a partner or a loved one can jump to conclusions that they are not loved, that the relationship has taken a downward turn or that they have done something wrong. For instance, a depressive may have difficulty talking or holding eye contact and this can tap into the vulnerabilities of those with whom they are most closely connected

- There can be a significant feeling of unfairness in a relationship when everything seems to be about the depressed person and their dark burdens. This can be worked through, but it is very important that a partner also expresses how they feel. The forgotten person in depression is very often the individual who lives with the depressed, and it is paramount that they also express their difficulties. If these are not expressed, this can lead to resentment and can create distance between individuals, which will only aggravate any difficulties in the relationship

- It can sometimes happen that a partner who is comfortable living with a depressed individual can become uneasy when the depression lifts. In this case, they probably need to seek therapy themselves

As depressives, we can engage in behaviour that can affect the quality of a healthy relationship:

- Fixation on self
- Taking life and self too seriously
- Isolation from and over-dependence on others
- Excessive worry; excessive guilt
- Dishonesty
- Neglect of partner
- Seeing only the negative; no acknowledgement of the positive
- Procrastination
- Social anxiety
- Fear of hurt, failure, rejection or commitment
- Unrealistic expectations

- Perfectionism
- Oversensitivity
- Avoidance of criticism or confrontation
- Manipulation
- Feeling like a victim
- Lack of assertiveness
- Comparing themselves to others
- Stereotyping
- Rigidity or controlling tendencies, or the opposite
- Indecisiveness and not keeping arrangements
- People-pleasing or approval-seeking
- Jealousy and resentment
- Passivity and denial of own needs
- Nondisclosure of self
- Aggressiveness

It can be helpful to recognise our destructive behaviours and patterns that may affect the quality of our relationships. By doing so, we can begin to learn healthier and more productive ways of relating to others. Below is a list of behaviours that are characteristic of a more healthy relationship:

- Open communication and tolerance
- Trust in and tolerance of each other
- Encouragement and acceptance of each other
- Willingness to be vulnerable

- Individuality and balance of closeness and aloneness
- Assertiveness
- No attempts to control, fix or manipulate
- Flexibility and forgiveness of self and other
- Honesty and loyalty
- Consistency in terms of commitment
- Sharing of self
- Acceptance of mistakes
- Willingness to take risks and learn from them
- Fairness and respect
- Personal growth encouragement of each other's interests
- Concern and interest in each other's lives
- Willingness to have fun and relax
- Humility and ability to accept feedback
- Dealing with difficulties and resolving them
- Responsibility for self
- Maintaining a balance of giving and receiving

Some More Ideas to Keep Depression at Bay

Preventing depression from returning is an ongoing endeavour; it requires effort, awareness and creativity.
Below are some more ideas for continued recovery:

- Continue routines even when you feel good
- Keep regular appointments for the dentist, doctor, optician, etc.

- Involve yourself in at least one meaningful cause
- Stay healthy: exercise, eat fresh foods, control alcohol, drink plenty of water, etc.
- Engage in activities that give you a sense of joy, fulfilment and purpose
- Make time for solitude
- Don't sweat the small stuff
- Be kind
- Surround yourself with positive people and optimistic friends, associates and relatives who possess a healthy sense of humour and who nurture friendships
- Give and receive affection
- Actively manage your stress
- Challenge yourself to develop or learn new skills, hobbies, languages, sports or other interests
- Find support and give it back
- Engage with nature each week; go for a walk, do the gardening or just appreciate the plants around you or the sky above you
- Too much daydreaming can be detrimental but the right balance can be of benefit
- Listen to your inner voice; it can speak to you through hunches, gut feelings, impulses and thoughts
- Use self-affirmations
- Get daily or weekly spiritual nourishment
- Release uncomfortable emotions
- Cut your losses and move on from mistakes, tragedies or setbacks

- Continue to identify other supports and how to access them, e.g. pets
- Use and take part in community resources such as libraries, volunteer groups, support groups, etc.
- Build on what works in terms of coping with and preventing depression and fine-tune what doesn't; don't discard a technique out of hand as it may work again
- It's trial and error; every effort counts

It may be advisable to keep writing a journal or progress reports as they can be very helpful in identifying new and more positive behaviours.

Summary

- Seeking help, preferably professional help, is the best course of action, and identifying and challenging any barriers you might have to this may be necessary
- Continued recovery requires continued effort
- By being aware of the signs of relapse we may then be able to interrupt a developing depression
- Effective time management, sleeping soundly and meditation are reported by many as a great benefit in continued recovery
- Living with a depressive can be very challenging, so attention needs to be given towards developing and maintaining a healthy relationship
- Be creative with your ideas for continued recovery and keeping depression at bay

Example of an Awareness Journal

	Situation, Date/Time	Physical Surroundings	Body's Reaction	Behaviours	Emotions	Self-Talk	Result
What happened	11/09/2010 12:45 p.m. – spoke to an old boss	At home, on telephone, with radio on in the background	Hungry; tense; butterflies in stomach	Over-explained myself; defensive; tried too hard to impress	Nervous; annoyed; frustrated	Put myself down; very self-critical	Low self-esteem; low self-confidence; irritated
What I can do the next time	Ring after lunch when he's not hungry	No change	Deep breathing to relax before and during talk	More assertive; be clear and concise; leave silences	Confident; assured	I did the best that I could	Happy; competent; capable; calm

165

Conclusion

This book has many suggestions for how to manage your depression, but it is vital that you adapt these ideas to your own needs and that you become creative in finding what best suits your requirements. It is natural that we may lose our energy and we may feel low at times, but remember that we can help ourselves. Also, our emotions will change over time as nothing ever stays the same.

It is possible to achieve a more manageable depression that can affect us less and less over time and can become lower in its intensity. If I can learn to manage my own depression then I believe that everyone is also able to learn to manage theirs. There is hope!

Although we may still get a debilitating hit of darkness every now and then, it is important to remember that we are not back at the beginning. The work we have done and the energy we have put into ourselves will still have a positive effect. Just refocus on your exercises, methods and coping skills and remember: *make the effort.*

References

Badner, J.A. and Gershon, E.S. (2002), 'Meta-analysis of whole-genome linkage scans of bipolar disorder and schizophrenia', *Molecular Psychiatry*, 7, 405–411.

Beck, A.T. (1967), *Depression: Clinical, Experimental and Theoretical Aspects*, New York: Harper & Row.

Beck, A.T., Steer, R.A., Kovacs, M. and Garrison, B. (1985), 'Hopelessness and eventual suicide: A 10-year prospective study of patients hospitalized with suicidal ideation', *American Journal of Psychiatry*, 142, 559–563.

Brown, G.M. and Andrews, B. (1986), 'Social support and depression' in R. Trumbell and H.M. Appley (eds.), *Dynamics of Stress: Physiological, Psychological and Social Perspectives*, New York: Plenum, 257–282.

Connolly, J.F. (1998), *Suicide – Human Tragedy, Global Responsibility*, The Irish Association of Suicidology, report of the second public meeting.

Connolly, J.F. (1996), *Suicide in Ireland: A Growing Problem*, The Irish Association of Suicidology, report of the first public meeting.

Durkheim, E. (1952), *Suicide: A Study in Sociology*, trans. Spaulding, J. and Simpson, G., London: Routledge and Kegan Paul.

Egan, M. (1997), *Suicide: A Tragedy*, Garda Síochána College, Student/probation school, phase 2, policing studies project.

Egeland, J.A., Gerhard, D.S., Pauls, D.L. et al. (1987), 'Bipolar affective disorders linked to DNA markers on chromosome 11', *Nature*, 325, 783–787.

Government of Ireland (2001), *Suicide in Ireland: A National Study*, Dublin: Department of Public Health.

Government of Ireland (1998), *Report of the National Task Force on Suicide*, Dublin: Departments of Public Health on Behalf of the Chief Executive Officers of the Health Boards.

Harris, E.C. and Barraclough, B. (1997), 'Suicide as an outcome for mental disorders', *British Journal of Psychiatry*, 170, 205–228.

McKeon, P. (1998), *Suicide in Ireland: A Global Perspective and a National Strategy*, Dublin: Aware Publications.

Moore, P., Landolt, H.P., Seifritz, E., et al. (2000), 'Clinical and physiological consequences of rapid tryptophan depletion', *Neuropsychopharmacology*, 23, 601–622.

National Office for Suicide Prevention (2008), *Annual Report: Reducing Suicide Requires a Collective, Concerted Effort from All Groups in Society*, Dublin: Health Service Executive.

Nowlan, D. (1998), paper given at the Third Annual Conference on Suicide Prevention, Irish Association of Suicidology.

O'Neill, J.M. (1982), 'Gender and sex role conflict and strain in men's lives: Implications for psychiatrists, psychologists and other human services providers', in K. Solomon and N. Levy (eds.), *Men in Transition: Theory and Therapy*, New York: Plenum Press, 5–44.

O'Neill, J.M., Good, G.E. and Holmes, S. (1995), 'Fifteen years of research on men's gender role conflict: New paradigms for empirical research', in R. Levent and W. Pollack (eds.), *Foundations for a New Psychology for Men*, New York: Basic Books, 164–206.

Pallis, D., Gibbons, J. and Pierce, D. (1984), 'Estimating suicide risk among attempted suicides. II. Efficiency of predictive scales after the attempt', *British Journal of Psychiatry*, 141, 37–44.

Schotte, D.E. and Clum, G.A. (1982), 'Suicide ideation in a college population: A test of a model', *Journal of Consulting and Clinical Psychology*, 50, 690–696.

Seligman, M.E.P. (1974), 'Depression and learned helplessness' in R.J. Friedman and M.M. Katz (eds.), *The Psychology of Depression: Contemporary Theory and Research*, Washington, DC: Winston-Wiley, 83–113.

Index